E-COMMERCE
IN CAREC COUNTRIES
LAWS AND POLICIES

AUGUST 2021

Contents

Tables

Acknowledgments

This study under the Central Asia Regional Economic Cooperation (CAREC) Program is an outcome of collaborative effort between the Asian Development Bank (ADB) and CAREC Institute (CI), under the supervision of Emma Fan, director of Public Management, Financial Sector and Regional Cooperation (EAPF) Division of ADB's East Asia Department (EARD) and Syed Shakeel Shah, director of CI.

The support and overall guidance of M. Teresa Kho, director general of ADB's EARD throughout the production is gratefully acknowledged.

The study team was led by Dorothea Lazaro (regional cooperation specialist, EAPF, ADB) and Iskandar Abdullaev (deputy director 2, CI). The study builds on a comprehensive assessment delivered by John Gregory (lead author) to the CAREC Institute in March 2020 and updated with recent legislations and data available online as of March 2021.

EAPF consultants Loreli de Dios, Camille Cyn Isles, Julius Irving Santos, and Aiken Rose Tafgar, and CI's Qaisar Abbas and Tumurpurev Dulambazar provided technical and research support.

Valuable comments and suggestions were received from ADB staff: Saad Paracha and Lyaziza Sabyrova of Central and Central and West Asia Regional Department (CWRD), Jong Woo Kang and James Villafuerte of Economic Research and Regional Cooperation Department, and Seok Yong Yoon and Yuebin Zhang of Sustainable Development and Climate Change Department. Technical advice was provided by Luca Castellani of United Nations Commission on International Trade Law, and Yann Duval, Soo Hyun Kim and Tengfei Wang, of United National Economic and Social Commission for Asia and the Pacific.

CAREC Program advisors and regional cooperation coordinators assisted in collecting data and legislative updates, namely: Ahmad Farid Amiri and Farahmand Ahmadi from Afghanistan, Ashraf Kuliyev from Azerbaijan, Chaoyi Hu from People's Republic of China, Ekaterine Koroshinadze from Georgia, Diyar Tassym and Guldana Sadykova from Kazakhstan, Meder Turgunbekov and Aidana Berdybekova from the Kyrgyz Republic, Amarjargal Delgersaikhan from Mongolia, Ganjina Fazilova from Tajikistan, Durdy Ilamanov from Turkmenistan, and Nadir Safaev and Rovshan Mamurov from Uzbekistan. The study benefited from discussions with CAREC delegates who participated at the *CAREC Webinar on E-Commerce and Paperless Trade* held on 3 September 2020.

Richard Vokey and Jason Beerman supported content review and copyediting. Jan Carlo Dela Cruz created the cover art and Edith Creus did the typesetting. The Department of Communications provided support for publishing the report. CWRD's Sarah Cueno and Honey May Manzano-Guerzon, and EARD's Desi Arvin Diaz, Genny Mabunga, Edith Joan Nacpil, Sophia Castillo-Plaza, and Angeli Vega supported the publication process.

The study is supported by ADB's Technical Assistance (TA) 9712: Implementing the Integrated Trade Agenda in the CAREC Program, cofinanced by the Regional Cooperation and Integration Fund and the People's Republic of China Poverty Reduction and Regional Cooperation Fund (PRCF) and TA 8301: CAREC – Supporting Capacity Development Needs of CAREC 2020 (also cofinanced by PRCF).

Abbreviations

ADB	Asian Development Bank
B2B	business-to-business
B2C	business-to-consumer
CAREC	Central Asia Regional Economic Cooperation
COVID-19	coronavirus disease
CSC	certification service center
CSP	certification service provider
EAEU	Eurasian Economic Union
ECAC	Electronic Certification Accreditation Council
ECC	United Nations Convention on the Use of Electronic Communications in International Contracts
ESCAP	Economic and Social Commission for Asia and the Pacific
EU	European Union
GDPR	General Data Protection Regulation
ICT	information and communication technology
MLEC	Model Law on Electronic Commerce
MLES	Model Law on Electronic Signatures
OECD	Organisation for Economic Co-operation and Development
PRC	People's Republic of China
PKI	public key infrastructure
UN	United Nations

UN/CEFACT	United Nations Centre for Trade Facilitation and Electronic Business
UNCITRAL	United Nations Commission on International Trade Law
UNCTAD	United Nations Conference on Trade and Development
UNNExT	United Nations Network of Experts for Paperless Trade and Transport in Asia and the Pacific
WCO	World Customs Organization
WIPO	World Intellectual Property Organization
WTO	World Trade Organization

Executive Summary

Most of the world today communicates electronically. The share of global trade conducted online is growing, offering benefits both domestically and internationally. Digital trade is improving the efficiency of domestic economies and creating new jobs, thereby helping developing economies and least-developed countries narrow development gaps and the rural–urban divide. The coronavirus disease (COVID-19) pandemic and changing global landscape have heightened the need to facilitate digital trade.

However, the commercial laws governing these electronic commerce (e-commerce) transactions have not always kept up with the new realities. The countries that have amended their national laws with e-commerce in mind have often taken different paths. In an era of global and regional economic blocs, these differences can create inefficiencies or barriers to trade.

This study aims to explain the legal and policy issues that affect e-commerce development among member countries of the Central Asia Regional Economic Cooperation (CAREC) Program and to improve the understanding and receptiveness of governments to constructive and coordinated reforms. Legislative and regulatory texts available online and with English translation as of December 2019 from all CAREC countries (and few updates from 2020) relating to electronic transactions (e-transactions), privacy, cybercrime, and consumer protection were reviewed.

Policy Context Aside from the Legal Regime

Some collateral issues—beyond the scope of this study—are important for CAREC countries policy makers to consider including:

- **The key element of attitudes and trust.** Popular attitudes to technology and to commerce generally can affect social or cultural acceptance of e-transactions.
- **Seeking the right balance in regulation.** CAREC countries must also strike a balance between the promotion of private choices and the protection of public policy goals.
- **Having the tools to effectively apply e-commerce law.** State power and efficient legal processes and institutions are needed to make good e-commerce laws work effectively, overcome social or cultural hesitation, and build trust in e-transactions.

Policy Options and Recommendations

Electronic Transactions

Technology Neutrality or Specificity?

The United Nations Commission on International Trade Law (UNCITRAL) has prepared influential legal texts to govern global e-commerce. UNCITRAL's guiding principle is technology neutrality, i.e., not specifying what technology should be used to achieve legal validity for commercial uses of electronic communications.

However, many states have found this approach insufficient to ensure what they considered the adequate reliability of the authentication of origin or integrity of electronic documents (e-documents). They have, as a result, required the use of a special kind of electronic signature (e-signature) known as a digital signature, which is created by a special kind of encryption.

CAREC countries may consider the following general legal approaches:

(i) **Technology neutrality.** This approach lets the law serve the commercial and security needs of transacting parties. The state need not be involved in prescribing technology that is bound to change over time.

(ii) **Technology specificity (use of digital signatures).** Technology specificity assists transacting parties, whether businesses or individuals, that do not have the capacity to judge the reliability of an e-signature or e-document.

(iii) **Hybrid law (with elements of both systems).** Some transacting parties do not need the full high-tech solutions and find it expensive and difficult. Some transactions may not justify its expense. However, other communications are particularly important (i.e., those involving public officials or very high-value transactions) and require more assurance of authenticity than a routine commercial deal.

Recommendation. CAREC countries should consider hybrid legislation that maximizes the autonomy of commercial parties to satisfy themselves on signature and document technology, while ensuring that official or vulnerable parties have legal and reliable electronic communications.

International Harmonization

CAREC countries' laws on e-commerce should be aligned with international standards, notably the following:

(i) **United Nations Convention on Contracts for the International Sale of Goods.** Originally adopted in 1980, this convention sets out basic rules of contract law for international sales of goods, which can apply to electronic sales.

(ii) **United Nations Framework Agreement on Facilitation of Cross-border Paperless Trade in Asia and the Pacific.** Without prescribing specific texts, this agreement sets out principles and priorities for member state legislation on cross-border e-commerce. Membership also provides opportunities for collaboration and mutual support in development of legal frameworks.

(iii) **United Nations Convention on the Use of Electronic Communications in International Contracts.** The convention, generally called the Electronic Communications Convention (ECC), sets out how electronic contracts can be integrated into the commercial laws of member states. It can be made to work as domestic law as well.

Recommendation. CAREC countries should harmonize their e-transactions laws, and those not yet members of these three United Nations conventions should accede to them.

Regulatory Matters

Privacy

Most CAREC countries have some form of privacy legislation. The laws tend to reflect the main points of the international standards: (i) that personal data should be collected only with the consent of the person it is about (the data subject), and for the purpose for which the consent was obtained; and (ii) that data should not be kept longer than necessary. The measures available to enforce these rights vary in scope and impact.

Recommendation. To protect the personal data of their residents both at home and when the data crosses national borders, CAREC countries should ensure that their privacy legislation is effective in practice and consistent with international best practices.

Cybercrime

The CAREC countries have long-standing laws governing such documentary crimes as fraud and forgery. Enforcing these laws does not depend on whether the offenses are committed by traditional means or by use of computers. However, computers have also permitted new kinds of criminal activity, notably interference with data and data flows. Intangibles such as data may not even be protected under traditional law.

Appropriate cybercrime laws cover offenses such as unauthorized access to a computer or a network, and theft of data. Infecting computers or networks with malware that harms or prevents their operation entirely should also be an offense. The provisions on cybercrime of most CAREC countries tend to cover these offenses. The countries that lack these provisions should enact them. Administrative cooperation with foreign investigations also needs to be ensured, since cybercriminals cross borders easily. International conventions are available as models for the offenses and appropriate cooperation.

Recommendation. CAREC countries should ensure that their laws prohibit the cybercrime activities listed in international conventions. Their ability to collaborate in international enforcement efforts—including through the exchange of data on local proceedings and local suspects—must be adequate to meet the challenges of cross-border cybercrime.

Consumer Protection

The other major barrier to creating consumer trust in e-commerce is inadequate consumer protection. Without legal protection, consumers may be unsure whether they will actually receive the goods and services that they buy online—and, if they do, whether they will have a remedy if what they receive is defective.

Although many CAREC countries have laws against fraud or misrepresentation that can be applied to consumer activity, few have adopted dedicated consumer protection laws. Those that exist vary. Some are modern, some out of date, and some incomplete.

States need to enforce the consumer rights they create. A number of methods exist to do so, such as consumer protection bureaus that review complaints and that are empowered to compel remedies and special tribunals (online or offline) to deal with low-value, high-volume disputes. States should not raise consumer expectations about protection that cannot be met. Governments should ensure that consumers are aware of their legal remedies.

Recommendation. CAREC countries should adopt consumer protection legislation that is consistent with the United Nations and Organisation for Economic Co-operation and Development (OECD) guidelines and models. They should pay particular attention to enforcing the legal rights this legislation is meant to provide.

Where to Go from Here

CAREC countries are at different stages in building their legislative frameworks for e-commerce. They need to cooperate with one another to maximize the consistency and harmonization of these legal frameworks in accordance with recognized international standards. CAREC countries should make it a collective priority to ensure that their laws support e-commerce both domestically and globally. This includes developing rules on privacy, cybercrime, and consumer protection.

Building or strengthening the role of institutions. National institutions may need to be strengthened to support e-commerce. This may include (i) establishing a dedicated multiministry task force with private sector participation, (ii) coordinating legal opinions about potential reforms to ensure that departments or agencies reach consistent positions, (iii) allowing all stakeholders to communicate electronically, (iv) replicating national work at the international level through technical and legal working groups and coordinating these two levels, and (v) working closely with development partners in acceding to international conventions related to e-commerce.

Stakeholder awareness and consultations. States should consult with and raise the awareness of e-commerce stakeholders through, among other things, surveys of business and trade associations or professional bodies. This could be particularly helpful in deciding which e-commerce transactions or documents should be authenticated as the transacting parties choose, and which should be subject to more objectively reliable technology-specific processes.

Participation in international agreements and forums for cooperation. Domestic e-commerce legislation must be accompanied by the implementation of instruments or international agreements relevant to trade or commerce. Besides those already mentioned, the World Trade Organization (WTO) Trade Facilitation Agreement obliges parties to transact public business (such as customs processing) electronically. CAREC countries could also consider participating in the international enforcement of consumer rights, including investigations through the International Consumer Protection and Enforcement Network.

Regional collaboration. CAREC countries should collaborate on and coordinate the progress and content of their e-commerce law reforms. Existing international and regional platforms, such as the CAREC Program, provide opportunities for knowledge and information sharing and could best promote regional harmonization of laws and mutual recognition. CAREC countries can learn from recent and emerging trade agreements that aim to reduce trade barriers in digital economy, facilitate interoperability and trust, and consider innovative regulatory areas for future cooperation. Furthermore, cross-border initiatives being undertaken under the CAREC Program to promote digital connectivity and interoperability between countries will lead to more inclusive e-commerce in the region and beyond.

1 Introduction

The long-term strategy for the Central Asia Regional Economic Cooperation (CAREC) Program—CAREC 2030—aims to make the program a strong catalyst of trade expansion and economic diversification.[1] The critical role of electronic commerce in linking CAREC countries with global value chains and diversifying economies has been further underscored in the CAREC Integrated Trade Agenda 2030, which was endorsed at the 17th Ministerial Conference on CAREC in 2018.[2] Promotion of e-commerce and innovation is an identified priority and common objective among the CAREC countries, especially with the rise of digital economies.

The disruptive effects of the coronavirus disease (COVID-19) pandemic have resulted in a global spike in business-to-consumer (B2C) sales as well as business-to-business (B2B) e-commerce transactions (WTO 2020).[3] Aside from highlighting the importance of digital technologies, the WTO note stated that the experiences and lessons learned from the crisis can incentivize and inform discussion and international cooperation to facilitate and encourage e-commerce, thereby increasing the cross-border movement of goods and services; narrowing digital divides; and leveling the playing field for micro, small, and medium-sized enterprises.[4]

The Asian Development Bank (ADB) and the United Nations (UN) Economic and Social Commission for Asia and the Pacific (ESCAP) 2018 report has identified three interrelated categories of factors that affect the development of an e-marketplace and a mature e-commerce ecosystem: (i) economic conditions, (ii) the legal and institutional environment, and (iii) social acceptance and awareness.[5]

This study focuses on an important aspect of the legal and institutional environment—the laws affecting electronic commerce in the CAREC countries. It asks, what is the legal environment now, and what should it be if it is to facilitate the growth of e-commerce in the region? The study begins with an overview of e-commerce activities in the 11 member countries of the CAREC Program: Afghanistan, Azerbaijan, Georgia, Kazakhstan, the Kyrgyz Republic, Mongolia, Pakistan, the People's Republic of China (PRC), Tajikistan, Turkmenistan, and Uzbekistan. This serves as a backdrop for discussing the opportunities and challenges that electronic communications present for the CAREC countries' legal regimes. The principal approaches taken internationally to govern e-transactions are considered, as well those adopted in the fields of personal privacy, consumer protection, cybersecurity, and cybercrime. The study then examines the current CAREC countries' laws in these domains and measures them against the recognized international standards. The study concludes with recommendations for developing the current CAREC legal regimes both domestically, and regionally to suit the world of e-commerce today and in the future. To do this, CAREC countries will need to further harmonize their legal regimes to make trade easier both within their borders and internationally.

---

[1]   Asian Development Bank (ADB). 2017. *CAREC 2030 Connecting the Region for Shared and Sustainable Environment.* Manila. https://www.adb.org/sites/default/files/institutional-document/383241/carec-2030.pdf.

[2]   ADB. 2018. *CAREC Integrated Trade Agenda 2030 and Rolling Strategic Action Plan 2018–2020.* Manila. https://www.adb.org/sites/default/files/institutional-document/490576/carec-trade-agenda-2030-action-plan-2018-2020.pdf.

[3]   Electronic commerce laws are generally applied without distinction and refer to both B2B and B2C e-commerce throughout the report except as otherwise reported in Chapter 2.

[4]   World Trade Organization (WTO). 2020. *E-Commerce, Trade and the COVID-19 Pandemic: Information Note.* Geneva. https://www.wto.org/english//tratop_e/covid19_e/ecommerce_report_e.pdf.

[5]   ADB and Economic and Social Commission for Asia and the Pacific (ESCAP). 2018. Embracing the E-Commerce Revolution in Asia and the Pacific. Manila. https://www.adb.org/sites/default/files/publication/430401/embracing-e-commerce-revolution.pdf.

2 Opportunities and Challenges of Electronic Communications

Information and communication technology (ICT) has expanded the opportunities for economic agents to initiate or participate in economic activity. The internet in particular has enabled producers to reach more markets and input sources. This has lowered costs, spurred innovation, given consumers wider choices, and affected trade substantially. As a result, almost all the Central Asia Regional Economic Cooperation (CAREC) governments have been pursuing national ICT or digital strategies to apply ICT in all areas of their economies. Between 2000 to 2006, some CAREC countries began to modernize their telecommunications infrastructure.[6]

Electronic commerce (e-commerce) —i.e., the sale or purchase of products and services via telecommunications networks—has been shown to raise efficiency and productivity. These are economic benefits all countries must be able to tap into.

While the coronavirus disease (COVID-19) pandemic has underlined the indispensable role of e-commerce, its burgeoning importance was evident long before the crisis erupted. The global value of e-commerce sales reached almost $26 trillion by 2018, which was equivalent to 30% of global gross domestic product according to estimates by the United Nations Conference on Trade and Development (UNCTAD).[7] Of this total, business-to-business (B2B) totaled $21 trillion, and business-to-consumer (B2C) $4.4 trillion. Almost 10% of B2C e-commerce crossed borders.[8]

Excluding the People's Republic of China (PRC), the number of e-commerce users in CAREC countries reached about 65.4 million in 2019. E-commerce user penetration was in the 23%–38% range in six countries, but only 16% in two. The PRC is the world's largest e-commerce market, with its 855.1 million e-commerce users representing a 61% penetration rate. In the PRC, the revenue per e-commerce user in 2019 was $1,008.80, compared with the global average of $607.07. The average for nine of the CAREC countries was $60.15, with revenue per user ranging from $21.50 to $129.26 across the group (Table 1).

The condition, quality, and level of development of internet infrastructure, e-payment systems, and delivery logistics are factors directly affecting the accessibility and viability of e-commerce activities.[9] These are considered in partly describing the state of CAREC countries' readiness for overall e-communications, and particularly e-commerce.

---

[6] An accompanying study examines e-commerce infrastructure covering internet infrastructure, payments, logistics, and e-commerce market in CAREC countries.

[7] The estimates were based on the ratios obtained from countries with data. UNCTAD has no country-specific estimates. UNCTAD. 2018. UNCTAD Estimates of Global E-commerce 2018. *UNCTAD Technical Notes on ICT for Development*. No. 15. https://unctad.org/system/files/official-document/tn_unctad_ict4d15_en.pdf.

[8] Based on the total B2C sales of the top 10 merchandise exporters ($404 billion).

[9] ADB and ESCAP (2018) considered economic factors and conditions as one of three groups of barriers and facilitators of e-commerce development. It encompasses affordability and access to ICT, bandwidth availability, online payment options, delivery infrastructure, and economies of scale (footnote 5).

Table 1: E-Commerce Use, 2019

Country	Number of Users (million)	User Penetration (% of population)	Average Revenue per User ($)
Afghanistan	n.a.	n.a.	n.a.
Azerbaijan	3.1	31	101.22
PRC	855.1	61	1,008.80
Georgia	1.3	35	78.03
Kazakhstan	7.0	38	129.26
Kyrgyz Republic	1.5	23	33.10
Mongolia	0.8	24	38.12
Pakistan	41.0	19	51.92
Tajikistan	1.4	15	21.60
Turkmenistan	0.9	15	21.50
Uzbekistan	8.5	25	42.32
CAREC-10[a]	65.4	21	60.15
All CAREC countries	920.5	54	941.42
World	3,170.8	41	607.07

CAREC = Central Asia Regional Economic Cooperation, n.a. = not available, PRC = People's Republic of China.

[a] CAREC-10 includes all countries in the CAREC Program except the PRC.

Note: E-commerce is one of six major business-to-commerce digital platforms, the other five being online travel, advertising technology, transportation, e-services, and digital media.

Source: ADB estimates based on Statista. 2020. *Statista Digital Market Outlook*. https://www https://www.statista.com/outlook/digital-markets.

Information and Communication Technology Infrastructure

ICT infrastructure refers to the telecommunications backbones and networks, equipment and devices, and protocols and procedures that enable users to interact. Change in this area is rapid. The reach and quality of internet infrastructure in CAREC countries vary widely, as may be gleaned from data on servers per population, bandwidth per user, and network coverage and speeds (Tables 2–4). Secure internet servers, as measured by the number of distinct publicly trusted secure sockets layer/transport layer security certificates, are dense by CAREC standards in Georgia, Kazakhstan, and Mongolia, but on a per-population basis represent only one-fourth of the world average of 10,000 per million. These servers are most scarce in Afghanistan, Pakistan, Tajikistan, and Turkmenistan.[10]

Domestic and international ICT infrastructure form the spine and building blocks of the internet. The bandwidth provided by this infrastructure affects the speed at which information travels between users and thus the quality of internet use and other international data connections. Among eight CAREC countries where data is available in 2018, Georgia has the highest international bandwidth per internet user.[11] At 140,194 bits per second, however, it was very low compared with the global average of 224,803 bits per second (Table 2). On the other hand,

---

[10] Secure sockets layer and transport layer security are protocols for data encryption and authentication that secure communications over the internet.

[11] Total used capacity of all international connections between countries for transmitting internet and other traffic, including fiber-optic cables, radio links, and traffic processed by satellite ground stations and teleports to orbital satellites.

mobile broadband network coverage is widespread among CAREC countries. At least 75% of the population are covered by third generation or 3G networks in nine countries, including six where coverage exceeds the global average of 86%. Half of the population are reached by fourth generation or 4G networks in eight countries, four of which exceed the global average of 69%.[12]

Table 2: Internet Infrastructure

Country	Secure Internet Servers per Million People, 2019	International Internet Bandwidth per Internet User, 2018 (bps)	3G Network Coverage, 2018 (% of population)	4G Network Coverage, 2018 (% of population)
Afghanistan	28	n.a.	30.3	14.9
Azerbaijan	369	52,143	95.0	48.1
PRC	735	27,722	98.0	99.0
Georgia	2,776	140,194	100.0	85.0
Kazakhstan	2,359	55,068	92.7	75.0
Kyrgyz Republic	288	47,864	75.0	50.0
Mongolia	1,690	22,399	95.0	27.3
Pakistan	63	20,854	78.5	54.7
Tajikistan	71	2,256	90.0	80.0
Turkmenistan	20	n.a.	n.a.	67.0
Uzbekistan	453	n.a.	75.0	43.0
CAREC-10[a]	812	n.a.	73.0	55.0
All CAREC countries	805		75.0	59.0
World	10,050	224,803	86.0	69.0

bps = bits per second, CAREC = Central Asia Regional Economic Cooperation, PRC = People's Republic of China, 3G = third generation, 4G = fourth generation

[a] CAREC-10 includes all countries in the CAREC Program except the PRC.

Sources: World Bank, World Development Indicators. https://databank.worldbank.org/source/world-development-indicators (accessed 1 August 2020); Portulans Institute. 2019. The Network Readiness Index 2019: Towards a Future-Ready Society. Washington DC. https://networkreadinessindex.org/wp-content/uploads/2020/03/The-Network-Readiness-Index-2019-New-version-March-2020.pdf; and Global System for Mobile Communications Association. Mobile Connectivity Index 2019. https://www.mobileconnectivityindex.com/ (accessed 1 August 2020).

Table 3: International Connectivity Modes and Network Technologies

Country	International Connectivity Mode in 2019	3G Network	4G Network	5G Launch Year
Afghanistan	Satellite, fiber optics	UMTS 1900, UMTS 2100		
Azerbaijan	Satellite, fiber optics	UMTS 2100	LTE 1800	2022
PRC	Submarine cable, satellite, fiber optics	UMTS 2100		
Georgia	Submarine cable, fiber optics	UMTS 2100	LTE 800, LTE 1800	2023
Kazakhstan		UMTS 2100	LTE 800, LTE 1800, LTE 2100	2021

continued on next page

[12] All mobile broadband systems are based on the International Telecommunications Union's International Mobile Telecommunications (IMT) standards, which are specifications and requirements for high-speed service. Third generation or 3G technology must meet the IMT-2000 standard, with a cellular data transfer rate of 128–144 kilobits per second for high mobility and 384 kilobits per second for low mobility; for fixed wireless local area networks, the speed goes beyond 2 megabits per second. Fourth generation or 4G technologies that meet IMT-Advanced standards are Long-Term Evolution-Advanced and Wireless Metropolitan Area Networks-Advanced.

Table 3 *continued*

Country	International Connectivity Mode in 2019	3G Network	4G Network	5G Launch Year
Kyrgyz Republic	Satellite, fiber optics	UMTS 2100	LTE 2600	2024
Mongolia	Satellite, fiber optics	UMTS 2100		
Pakistan	Submarine cable, satellite, fiber optics	UMTS 850, UMTS 900, UMTS 2100	LTE 850, LTE 1800	
Tajikistan		UMTS 2100		2024
Turkmenistan		UMTS 2100	LTE 2600 (7)	2024
Uzbekistan	Satellite, fiber optics	UMTS 2100	LTE 700, LTE 2600, LTE 2700	2024

3G = third generation, 4G = fourth generation, 5G = fifth generation, LTE = Long-Term Evolution, PRC = People's Republic of China, UMTS = Universal Mobile Telecommunications System.

Note: Submarine communication cables on the seabed transmit 99% of international data worldwide. Fiber optics refer to thin glass wires inside a larger protective cable that transfer data through light signals. Satellites transmit data via radio waves.

Sources: International Telecommunications Union. ICT Eye. https://www.itu.int/net4/ITU-D/icteye/#/ (accessed 31 July 2020); GSMARENA. Country Reports. https://www.gsmarena.com/network-bands.php3 (accessed 1 August 2020).

Table 4: Internet Download Speeds, 2020 (Mbps)

Country	Mobile Download Speed	Fixed Broadband Download Speed
Afghanistan	5.52	7.38
Azerbaijan	30.99	21.24
PRC	103.67	133.60
Georgia	27.72	26.19
Kazakhstan	21.25	46.31
Kyrgyz Republic	20.06	40.26
Mongolia	19.19	35.63
Pakistan	14.86	8.87
Tajikistan	12.62	27.59
Turkmenistan		3.69
Uzbekistan	11.78	28.52
CAREC-10[a]	18.22	24.57
All CAREC countries	26.77	34.48
World	34.67	78.26

CAREC = Central Asia Regional Economic Cooperation, Mbps = megabits per second, PRC = People's Republic of China.

[a] CAREC-10 includes all countries in the CAREC Program except the PRC.

Source: Speedtest Global Index. https://www.speedtest.net/global-index (accessed 11 June 2020).

The availability and affordability of bandwidth are reflected in the levels of internet use and subscriptions to mobile cellular telephones and broadband internet (Tables 5 and 6). The PRC had 854.5 million internet users in 2019. For the other CAREC members, about 137 million people (or half of the overall CAREC population) were also using the internet. Pakistan, with 76 million users, had the largest share among the 10 CAREC countries outside of the PRC—the CAREC-10. Internet access at home was possible for 41% of households in the CAREC-10 and 35% had a computer, which in both cases were below the global averages. The flexibility of mobile access to the internet makes it highly popular, and mobile broadband subscriptions outnumbered fixed broadband subscriptions significantly in all the CAREC countries in 2018.

Table 5: Internet Access and Usage

Country	Internet Users, 2019 (million)	Internet Penetration, 2019 (% of population)	Households with Internet Access, 2018 (% of households)	Households with a Computer, 2018 (% of households)	Mobile Connections, 2019 (million)
Afghanistan	7.65	20	6	3.43	26.92
Azerbaijan	8.05	80	78	64.10	11.29
PRC	854.50	59	60	55.00	1,610.00
Georgia	2.70	68	70	62.11	5.57
Kazakhstan	14.73	79	88	78.50	25.45
Kyrgyz Republic	3.06	47	21	23.29	9.73
Mongolia	2.20	68	23	36.45	4.42
Pakistan	76.38	35	22	16.15	164.90
Tajikistan	2.42	26	12	14.83	10.04
Turkmenistan	1.56	26	11	10.73	4.79
Uzbekistan	18.34	55	80	38.50	25.14
CAREC-10[a]	137.09	50	41	35.00	288.25
All CAREC countries	991.59	51	43	37.00	1,898.25
World	4,540.00	59	55	47.10	7,950.00

CAREC = Central Asia Regional Economic Cooperation, PRC = People's Republic of China.

[a] CAREC-10 includes all countries in the CAREC Program except the PRC.

Sources: Kemp, Simon. 2020. Digital 2020. Afghanistan. https://datareportal.com/reports/digital-2020-afghanistan; Kemp, Simon. 2020. Digital 2020: Azerbaijan. https://datareportal.com/reports/digital-2020-azerbaijan; Kemp, Simon. 2020. Digital 2020: China. https://datareportal.com/reports/digital-2020-china; Kemp, Simon. 2020. Digital 2020: Georgia. https://datareportal.com/reports/digital-2020-georgia; Kemp, Simon. 2020. Digital 2020: Kazakhstan. https://datareportal.com/reports/digital-2020-kazakhstan; Kemp, Simon. 2020. Digital 2020: Kyrgyzstan. https://datareportal.com/reports/digital-2020-kyrgyzstan; Kemp, Simon. 2020. Digital 2020: Mongolia. https://datareportal.com/reports/digital-2020-mongolia; Kemp, Simon. 2020. Digital 2020: Pakistan. https://datareportal.com/reports/digital-2020-pakistan; Kemp, Simon. 2020. Digital 2020: Tajikistan. https://datareportal.com/reports/digital-2020-tajikistan; Kemp, Simon. 2020. Digital 2020: Turkmenistan. https://datareportal.com/reports/digital-2020-turkmenistan; Kemp, Simon. 2020. Digital 2020: Uzbekistan. https://datareportal.com/reports/digital-2020-uzbekistan (accessed 3 August 2020); and International Telecommunications Union. ICTEye. Country profile. https://www.itu.int/net4/itu-d/icteye/CountryProfile.aspx (accessed 3 August 2020).

Table 6: Subscriptions to Mobile Cellular Telephones and Broadband Internet, 2018

Country	Subscriptions per 100 People		
	Mobile Cellular	Fixed Broadband	Mobile Broadband
Afghanistan	59	0.05	19
Azerbaijan	104	18.20	60
PRC	115	28.54	95
Georgia	133	21.00	45
Kazakhstan	142	13.44	78
Kyrgyz Republic	123	3.81	94
Mongolia	133	9.66	84
Pakistan	73	0.85	29
Tajikistan	112	0.07	23

continued on next page

Table 6 *continued*

Country	Subscriptions per 100 People		
	Mobile Cellular	Fixed Broadband	Mobile Broadband
Turkmenistan	163	0.09	15
Uzbekistan	76	12.70	62
CAREC-10[a]	112	7.99	51
All CAREC countries	112	9.85	55
World	104	13.60	62

CAREC = Central Asia Regional Economic Cooperation, PRC = People's Republic of China.

[a] CAREC-10 includes all countries in the CAREC Program except the PRC. Average is 111.7.

Source: International Telecommunications Union. Country ICT Data. https://www.itu.int/en/ITU-D/Statistics/Pages/stat/default.aspx (accessed 3 August 2020).

E-Payment Systems

The ability to send and receive payments through electronic means is a critical requirement of e-commerce. E-payment systems allow payments to be made and controlled regardless of time or place. These may be card-based, electronic check, account transfer, electronic cash, or mobile payment systems. The many methods becoming increasingly available in CAREC countries include the use of digital mobile banking applications, credit and debit cards, e-purses, point-of-sale terminals, and third-party merchants. Some governments, like the Government of Azerbaijan, have programs to promote expansion and use of digital payments, transparency, and reduction of cash-related transactions costs among banks and businesses.

On average, 29% of the population aged 15 and over in the CAREC-10 countries and 32% in all CAREC countries overall had a debit card and thus the ability to make e-payments in 2017.[13] The percentages in Mongolia and the PRC exceeded the global average. Credit card ownership was much less prevalent. Only 10% of the total CAREC-10 population used the internet to make a purchase or pay bills online or used a mobile phone or the internet to access an account at a financial institution. A considerably higher proportion made or received digital payments (Table 7).

Table 7: Electronic Payment Capacity and Use, 2017
(%)

Country	Share of Respondents Who					
	Own a Debit Card	Own a Credit Card	Used a Debit or Credit Card to Make a Purchase	Used the Internet to Pay Bills or Purchase Online	Made or Received Digital Payments	Used Mobile Phone or Internet to Access Account
Afghanistan	2.7	1.1		0.5	10.8	0.9
Azerbaijan	24.6	5.3	7.4	9.4	24.6	2.0
PRC	66.8	20.8	41.9	48.8	67.9	39.8
Georgia	39.9	14.6	18.5	13.5	53.0	9.4
Kazakhstan	39.7	20.0	25.5	24.3	53.9	18.2
Kyrgyz Republic	19.3	3.6	6.7	5.0	36.1	5.8

continued on next page

---

[13]   The CAREC-10 countries refer to all countries in the CAREC Program except the PRC.

Table 7 *continued*

Country	Share of Respondents Who					
	Own a Debit Card	Own a Credit Card	Used a Debit or Credit Card to Make a Purchase	Used the Internet to Pay Bills or Purchase Online	Made or Received Digital Payments	Used Mobile Phone or Internet to Access Account
Mongolia	75.7	3.2	60.8	17.1	85.3	38.4
Pakistan	8.3	1.0		8.0	17.7	7.6
Tajikistan	15.9	5.7	10.8	12.8	43.9	8.3
Turkmenistan	37.9		5.6	2.0	34.3	2.2
Uzbekistan	24.1	0.6	25.0	7.1	34.2	6.7
CAREC-10[a]	28.8	6.1	20.0	10.0	39.4	10.0
All CAREC countries	32.3	7.6	22.5	13.5	42.0	12.7
World	47.7	18.4	32.6	29.0	52.3	24.9

CAREC = Central Asia Regional Economic Cooperation, PRC = People's Republic of China.
[a] CAREC-10 includes all countries in the CAREC Program except the PRC.
Source: World Bank. DataBank. Global Financial Inclusion. https://databank.worldbank.org/reports.aspx?source=global-financial-inclusion (accessed 7 August 2020).

Credit or debit cards are the main payment methods in Georgia, where PayPal is also popular. In the PRC, mobile digital systems Alipay and WeChat are widely used.[14] The Kyrgyz Republic is making advancements in mobile payment systems, and online payment in Uzbekistan is through the use of bank cards linked to smartphones. Mongolian commercial banks offer a wide range of online payment options. Larger e-commerce companies in Pakistan are starting to utilize digital payments. Online trade in Tajikistan is conducted through the national payment system. Cash payments are still preferred in Afghanistan, Azerbaijan, Kazakhstan, Pakistan, Turkmenistan, and Uzbekistan.[15]

Businesses with their own websites made up more than half (57%) of all the firms worldwide in 2018. Data available for seven CAREC countries showed a 44% average. The PRC led with 66% of its firms online, followed by the Kyrgyz Republic (57%), Georgia (49%), Pakistan (47%), and Kazakhstan (44%). About one-third of the firms in Azerbaijan, Mongolia, and Tajikistan had a presence on the internet.[16]

---

[14]   The PRC leads the world in online commercial activity. Of the world's 70 largest digital platforms, PRC-based platforms account for 22% of market capitalization value. Alibaba, Tencent, JD.com, and Baidu are also included in the Forbes' list of top 50 digital companies.
[15]   These are from country market analyses of Groupe Société Générale. Import Export Solutions. Country Profiles. https://import-export.societegenerale.fr/en/country (accessed 5 August 2020); and Government of the United States, Department of Commerce, International Trade Administration. 2 July 2019. *Azerbaijan – eCommerce*. https://www.export.gov/apex/article2?id=Azerbaijan-ecommerce; International Trade Administration, US Department of Commerce. 30 July 2019. *People's Republic of China – eCommerce*. https://www.export.gov/apex/article2?id=China-ecommerce. International Trade Administration, US Department of Commerce. 27 August 2019. *Georgia – eCommerce*. https://www.export.gov/apex/article2?id=Georgia-ECommerce; International Trade Administration, US Department of Commerce. 28 June 2019. *Kazakhstan – Direct Marketing*. https://www.export.gov/apex/article2?id=Kazakhstan-Direct-Marketing; International Trade Administration, US Department of Commerce. 2 August 2019. *Kyrgyz Republic – eCommerce*. https://www.selectusa.gov/article?id=Kyrgyz-Republic-Ecommerce; International Trade Administration, US Department of Commerce. 8 August 2017. *Mongolia – eCommerce*. https://www.export.gov/apex/article2?id=Mongolia-ECommerce; International Trade Administration, US Department of Commerce. 13 October 2019. *Pakistan: eCommerce*. https://www.trade.gov/knowledge-product/pakistan-ecommerce; International Trade Administration, US Department of Commerce. 15 February 2019. *Tajikistan – eCommerce*. https://www.export.gov/apex/article2?id=Tajikistan-ECommerce; International Trade Administration, US Department of Commerce. 21 July 2019. *Turkmenistan – eCommerce*. https://www.export.gov/apex/article2?id=Turkmenistan-ECommerce; International Trade Administration, US Department of Commerce. 3 July 2019. *Uzbekistan – eCommerce*. https://www.export.gov/apex/article2?id=Uzbekistan-ECommerce
[16]   Portulans Institute. 2019. The Networked Readiness Index 2019: Towards a Future-Ready Society., Washington DC. https://networkreadinessindex.org/wp-content/uploads/2020/03/The-Network-Readiness-Index-2019-New-version-March-2020.pdf.

Delivery Logistics

Goods purchased from abroad through B2B e-transactions are typically processed as regular imports. Meanwhile, most goods directly purchased by consumers through B2C e-transactions are delivered by postal services as direct mail or by commercial couriers.[17] This makes the postal service one of the pillars of successful e-commerce. The Universal Postal Union, a United Nations agency, analyzes the reliability and efficiency of postal operations based on the speed and predictability of delivery of items across all key segments of physical postal services (letter, parcel, and express package). CAREC countries have an average reliability score of 51, outperforming the world average of 49. By order of ranking, very high-scoring countries are Georgia, Azerbaijan, the PRC, Kazakhstan, and Pakistan. The performances of Mongolia and Uzbekistan come close to the world average as well. The bulk (83%) of the population in the eight CAREC countries where data is available have their mail delivered at home. This includes practically everyone in Georgia, Kazakhstan, the PRC, Pakistan, and Uzbekistan. The 2018 Logistics Performance Index rated all CAREC countries (except Azerbaijan) in several categories. On a scale of 1 to 5 (higher is better), their scores ranged from 1.80 to 3.75 for logistics infrastructure, from 1.92 to 3.59 for quality of logistics services, and from 2.38 to 3.84 for timeliness of shipments (Table 8).

Table 8: Postal and Logistics Performance Indexes, 2018

Country	Postal Reliability Score	Mail Delivered at Home (% of population)	LPI Score for Infrastructure Quality	LPI Score for Quality of Logistics Services	LPI Score for Timeliness of Shipments
Afghanistan	6	50	1.81	1.92	2.38
Azerbaijan	86				
PRC	85	99	3.75	3.59	3.84
Georgia	99	100	2.38	2.26	2.95
Kazakhstan	72	94	2.55	2.58	3.53
Kyrgyz Republic	20		2.38	2.36	2.94
Mongolia	47	51	2.10	2.21	3.06
Pakistan	54	95	2.20	2.59	2.66
Tajikistan	1	75	2.17	2.33	2.95
Turkmenistan			2.23	2.31	2.72
Uzbekistan	41	100	2.57	2.59	3.09
CAREC-10 countries	47	81	2.27	2.35	2.92
All CAREC countries	51	83	2.41	2.47	3.01
World	49	80			

CAREC = Central Asia Regional Economic Cooperation, CAREC-10 includes all countries in the CAREC Program except the PRC, LPI = Logistics Performance Index, PRC = People's Republic of China, UNCTAD = United Nations Conference on Trade and Development.
Note: The Postal Reliability Score ranges from 0 for worst to 100 for best. LPI scores range from 1 for very low to 5 for very high.
Sources: UNCTAD. 2019. UNCTAD B2C E-Commerce Index 2019. *UNCTAD Technical Notes on ICT for Development*. No. 14. https://unctad.org/system/files/official-document/tn_unctad_ict4d14_en.pdf; Universal Postal Union. Global or regional estimates. http://pls.upu.int/pls/ap/ssp_report.main2020?p_language=AN&p_choice=BROWSE (accessed 8 October 2020); Universal Postal Union. 2020. *Postal Development Report 2020*. https://www.upu.int/UPU/media/upu/publications/2020-Postal-Development-Report.pdf; and World Bank. LPI 2018. https://lpi.worldbank.org/international/global (accessed 8 August 2020).

---

[17]   These may be subsidiary logistics companies set up by e-commerce platforms and operators, global express companies whose main business is logistics rather than e-commerce, or national logistics companies that partner with international operators for last-mile delivery.

3 Framework for Electronic Communications Legislation

Electronic communications differ from communications on paper in important ways that have challenged the application of traditional rules of law to the former.

Invisible processes. Electronic communications are created through the use and interpretation of electronic signals. This provides numerous benefits to commerce and the public at large. The main challenge in law arises from the fact that the computations used to deliver text and numeric information are invisible. Users have to trust the computers involved to do it right, and to do it the same way every time—i.e., to display on the screen or to send to the printer the same text for every party to a transaction and everyone else with an interest in it, such as auditors, regulators, and tax authorities. However, bits and bytes can degrade or be changed undetectably, leaving the resulting screen or paper text looking as perfect as the original. This is not the case with paper, where it is very difficult to amend an original document without leaving a trace.

Legal uncertainties and doubts. Any user of a computer connected to a communications system may have cause to worry about intrusions into the computer for malicious or even criminal purposes. Consumers also wonder whether what they might buy online will be what is delivered to them, as well as whether they will have any remedy against a remote online merchant if the product that arrives is bad. The question for the merchants may be whether their remote online customers will pay them. The result of these and many other uncertainties have been unwillingness by some to trust electronic communications and e-commerce and a belief that the laws that apply to paper communications are inadequate to ensure confidence in the integrity of the products of electronic communications. When electronic communications first appeared in commerce, the existing laws protecting the integrity of paper documents did not fit them well and/or were difficult to apply. E-commerce transactions have expanded all over the world even in the absence of supporting legislation. The question here is how to remove the remaining barriers—those governing electronic transactions—and channel e-commerce in a way that encourages its growth in a safe, sustainable manner.

Removing Barriers to Electronic Transactions

The Model Law on Electronic Commerce

In 1996, the United Nations Commission on International Trade Law (UNCITRAL) adopted the Model Law on Electronic Commerce (MLEC), which has been enacted in more than 70 countries and remains the best template for e-commerce legal reforms.[18] Because it is a model law rather than a convention, the MLEC can

---

[18] United Nations Commission on International Trade Law. E-commerce documents: https://uncitral.un.org/en/texts/ecommerce; UNCITRAL. 1999. Model Law on Electronic Commerce with Guide to Enactment 1996. Vienna. https://uncitral.un.org/sites/uncitral.un.org/files/media-documents/uncitral/en/19-04970_ebook.pdf.

be applied by any legal system and adapted to fit into any legislative regime. The MLEC deals principally with form requirements, rather than with rules of substantive law. The MLEC also leaves a good deal of autonomy to transacting parties to decide how to satisfy its rules.

Electronic Documents

The main challenge to the validity and use of e-documents has often been legal requirements that certain documents be in writing. UNCITRAL's MLEC provides that electronic documents can satisfy that requirement when their information is accessible and usable for subsequent reference. Another barrier to the use of e-documents is the common requirement for the original versions of documents to be produced for legal purposes. The MLEC provides a method of analyzing information in electronic form to decide if it is a functional equivalent of a paper original, i.e., can the electronic version achieve the policy goal (the function) that lies behind the traditional legal rule? The key element for a functional equivalent to writing is whether the information can be shown to have retained its integrity from the time it was created until the time of analysis.

Electronic Signatures

Different legal systems give different weights to the importance of signatures, but all expect the connection between a legal or natural person and a document to be evidenced by the person's signature. Some countries consider the reliability of commercial signatures to be a matter decided by public policy and do not allow transacting parties to agree to their own standards. Where the law requires a signature, UNCITRAL's MLEC says that an electronic method of signing will be effective if it identifies the signatory, indicates the signatory's approval, and is as reliable as is appropriate in the circumstances. In many if not all Central Asia Regional Economic Cooperation (CAREC) countries, the law requires signatures for most transactions.

UNCITRAL added the Model Law on Electronic Signatures (MLES) in 2001 to help govern and build trust in the reliability of e-signatures. The MLES spelled out the characteristics of an e-signature that could be presumed to make it reliable. It also listed some rules regarding the liability and trustworthiness of the parties to e-signatures, including intermediaries who certify the identity of the users of e-signing devices. The MLES provisions have often inspired legislation in CAREC countries and elsewhere to support the mandatory or optional use of digital signatures (those created using cryptography) within the context of public key infrastructure (PKI).[19]

The MLES also provides a rule for recognizing electronic signatures generated in another country.[20] Countries that implement this model law are to give e-signatures of foreign origin legal effect to the extent that the foreign standards for issuing or recognizing e-signatures offer substantially the same degree of reliability as theirs. International rules and standards play a significant role in developing and maintaining a legal framework for electronic commerce.

The Role of the Private Sector

When weighing the roles of the private sector and state legislative and legal regimes in expanding e-commerce and their contribution to an economy, two issues stand out. The first is the ability of the private sector to conduct e-commerce without further reform. The second is the desirable degree of autonomy for the parties to e-commerce. Both involve assessments of risk and reward and the consideration of two basic questions:

---

[19]   Refers to the network of duties and functions of issuers and users of digital signatures and certificates.
[20]   UNCITRAL. 2002. UNCITRAL Model Law on Electronic Signatures with Guide to Enactment 2001. New York (Article 12). https://uncitral. un.org/sites/uncitral.un.org/files/media-documents/uncitral/en/ml-elecsig-e.pdf.

(i) **Is law reform necessary?** In many parts of the world, e-commerce grew before laws were changed. This growth was based on contracts between businesses (trading partner agreements) and on the flexibility of existing laws that allowed novelty. However, there were and are limits to how far private agreements could go to changing basic rules of law. Law reform was more economical of effort and more general of application than contractual regimes. The CAREC countries tended to leave little room for private initiative until the basic laws were enacted to allow for electronic documents and signatures. This study discusses further reforms that go beyond what transacting parties can do for themselves.

(ii) **How much regulation or party autonomy should there be?** The degree of regulation required by or wanted in a system greatly depends on the extent of risk the system is willing to tolerate. These risks fall into three broad categories:

   (a) *Risk to the transacting parties themselves.* Are the parties able and competent to make good decisions in novel areas? They may be free to fail, or the state may feel obliged to save them from bad choices. If the latter is the case, then the state is more likely to regulate the choices that lead to the risks.

   (b) *Risk to others.* A less regulated system may expose others potentially affected by business-to-business (B2B) or business-to-consumer (B2C) dealings to fraud or mistakes. Some societies are more willing than others to trust the competence and honesty of private actors; others rely on more extensive state oversight of economic activity.

   (c) *Risk to public policy.* Governments differ in how much uncertainty they can tolerate, and in deciding how much business failure should be allowed, and at what cost to the economy. Innovation has benefits and costs.

Risk tolerance differs between parties and states. It is a policy question, not a technical one, and law reform is a form of risk management that reflects this level of tolerance. In part to minimize on the need for state regulation, the CAREC countries may want to support the development of private sector capacities to manage risk. There is significant debate on e-commerce platforms' role in consumer protection. Over the years, big companies have continuously redefined their self-regulation policies to boost consumer confidence and mitigate consumers' distrust. For instance, Alibaba has introduced a third-party payment system, warranties on quality assurances, and online dispute resolution, and it has developed an intellectual property rights protection mechanism using advanced computing or big data. On the other hand, privacy and security issues are emerging with respect to these platforms because of unauthorized access or analysis of browsing behavior and shopping history of e-commerce users for targeted marketing or profiling.

Private technology will continue to offer new methods of doing e-commerce more securely. The law should leave room for the use of devices, codes, and platforms that are yet to be developed but could avoid the need for some state regulation or administrative supervision. It would be wise for CAREC countries to recognize the potential for private technology and allow them flexibility in the future to provide solutions to authentication questions. Continuing dialogue between the private and public sector, including development partners, is important. For example, the United Nations Conference for Trade and Development (UNCTAD) has launched the Business for eTrade Development platform, comprising a private sector advisory group, to optimize and support public policies for e-commerce development worldwide.

Regulation

UNCITRAL's work, especially on electronic documents and electronic signatures, has aimed to enable electronic transactions in a world full of requirements designed for paper documents. UNCITRAL does not attempt to propose rules of economic regulation for the world; there is too much local variation for such rules to have global application. However, its silence on such matters is not a statement by UNCITRAL that such regulation is not needed in order to facilitate electronic commerce.[21]

There are legal measures besides UNCITRAL's model laws that can build economic trust in electronic transactions. A 2018 report by the Asian Development Bank (ADB) and the United Nations Economic and Social Commission for Asia and the Pacific (ESCAP) and several other reports consistently mention the need for enabling a legal and institutional framework of e-commerce. This framework includes rules on privacy, consumer protection, and online security—the last equating to protection against cybercrime.[22] Such a framework builds crucial elements of the trust needed for e-commerce to grow.[23]

How effective these rules and regulations will be, however, depends on the ability of the state to administer and enforce them. The willingness of a country to reform its laws on e-commerce implies a willingness to get the state involved in ensuring that these reforms mean something in practice. If this does not happen, the trust required to support electronic transactions will not grow or be sustained.

Privacy

An individual's right to keep their personal information private has grown in the computer age. The most influential text of what one might consider the early computer era was a set of guidelines published by the Organisation for Economic Co-operation and Development (OECD) in 1980.[24] These guidelines have been made law in whole or in part by many countries to establish the following fundamental principles:

(i)   collection limitation (no more information should be collected than is needed for the purpose disclosed to the person providing the information),

(ii)   data quality (the information should be as reliable as possible),

(iii) purpose specification (the data collection must disclose to the data provider the purpose of the collection and proposed use of the data),

(iv)   use limitation (the data should not be used for any purpose other than what has been disclosed),

(v)   security safeguards (the data should be kept and managed securely),

(vi)   openness (the practices and policies of the data collectors should be knowable to those they affect),

(vii) individual participation (the people whose information is being collected and used should have the right to know what information is held and to have it corrected if appropriate), and

(viii) accountability (there should be an effective remedy for an individual for any breach of these rules by the data collector or user).

The OECD reviewed and revised the guidelines in 2013, while retaining many of the original principles.[25] Among the significant changes were greater emphasis on implementing and enforcing the principles and a focus on the

21   UNCITRAL. 1999. *Model Law on Electronic Commerce with Guide to Enactment 1996.* Vienna (paras. 13–14). https://uncitral.un.org/sites/uncitral.un.org/files/media-documents/uncitral/en/19-04970_ebook.pdf.

22   Footnote 5. See also United Nations Conference on Trade and Development (UNCTAD). 2019. Rapid eTrade Readiness Assessments of Least Developed Countries: Policy Impact and Way Forward. https://unctad.org/en/PublicationsLibrary/dtlstict2019d7_en.pdf; and United Nations (UN). 2019. *Digital and Sustainable Trade Facilitation: Global Report 2019.* https://www.unescap.org/sites/default/d8files/knowledge-products/UNtfsurvey%20global%20report%202019.pdf.

23   That said, laws to remove legal barriers to the use of e-communications can also be seen as building trust, especially where the law touches on authentication. J. Gregory. 2014. Legislating Trust, *Canadian Journal of Law and Technology.* 12 (1). https://digitalcommons.schulichlaw.dal.ca/cjlt/vol12/iss1/1/.

24   OECD. 1980 (amended 2013). *Guidelines on the Protection of Privacy and Transborder Flows of Personal Data.* https://www.oecd.org/internet/ieconomy/oecdguidelinesontheprotectionofprivacyandtransborderflowsofpersonaldata.htm.

25   OECD. 2013. *The OECD Privacy Framework.* https://www.oecd.org/sti/ieconomy/oecd_privacy_framework.pdf.

cross-border flow of personal information that reflects the advances in global information networks and the economic value of data. Inspired by the 1980 OECD guidelines, the Council of Europe strengthened privacy protection by adopting the Convention for the Protection of Individuals with regard to Automatic Processing of Personal Data, which was updated in 2018 to reflect the revision of the OECD guidelines.[26] Azerbaijan and Georgia, members of the Council of Europe, have adopted the 1981 version of this convention.

The third important source of thinking on and rules for protecting privacy (after the OECD Guidelines and the Council of Europe conventions, both as updated) is the 2016 General Data Protection Regulation (GDPR) of the European Union (EU), which came into force in 2018.[27] The GDPR not only governs the internal data practices of the EU, one of the world's largest economies, but the regulation also has spillover effects by applying to the personal data that EU member states transfer to the rest of the world. Data collection by international companies in the EU is also governed by the GDPR. These companies include many American and Asian businesses. Kazakhstan has announced that it will follow the GDPR in its administration of privacy legislation.[28] Georgia has an agreement with the EU that involves conforming with the GDPR as well.[29] The basic obligations that the GDPR imposes on data controllers in the public and private sectors are largely consistent with those that the OECD originally published in 1980.[30]

Cybercrime

Another vital ingredient of public confidence in e-commerce is an expectation of honest conduct online. This study assumes that the CAREC members have basic criminal laws in place prohibiting the usual forms of dishonesty, such as misrepresentation, fraud, forgery, and theft. Some countries also have competition laws meant to inhibit the creation of monopolies and monopoly-like conduct through such activities as price-fixing, price discrimination, and bait-and-switch selling. These laws are generally media-neutral: they apply to online and offline transactions equally. New legislation is not usually needed.[31] Adding protections that cover online crime aims to bolster the trust of consumers and business participants in e-commerce.[32]

The essential provisions of laws against cybercrime are widely agreed. The two treaties on the topic—one in place, one in draft form—have many common elements but take different approaches to administration. The Council of Europe Convention on Cybercrime (Budapest Convention of 2001) is very clear on the application of criminal law to online activity.[33] It aims to ensure that the 47 Council of Europe member states ban certain kinds of undesirable online conduct that might not be illegal under traditional law.[34]

---

[26] Council of Europe. 1981. *Convention for the Protection of Individuals with regard to Automatic Processing of Personal Data.* https://www.coe.int/en/web/conventions/full-list/-/conventions/treaty/108; and Council of Europe. 2018. Modernised Convention for the Protection of Individuals with Regard to the Processing of Personal Data. https://www.coe.int/en/web/data-protection/convention108/modernised.

[27] European Parliament and Council of European Union. 2016. *General Data Protection Regulation.* https://eur-lex.europa.eu/legal-content/EN/TXT/PDF/?uri=CELEX:32016R0679&from=EN. The GDPR replaced the influential EU Data Protection Directive of 1995.

[28] Government of Kazakhstan. Electronic government of the Republic of Kazakhstan. Cybersecurity. https://egov.kz/cms/en/cyberspace.

[29] European Commission. 2014. *Association Agreement between the European Union and the European Atomic Energy Community and their Member States, of the one part, and Georgia, of the other part.* https://eur-lex.europa.eu/legal-content/EN/TXT/?uri=CELEX:02014A0830(02)-20180601 (accessed August 2020).

[30] See footnote 27. See also EU GDPR Academy. Full text of EU GDPR (General Data Protection Regulation). https://advisera.com/eugdpracademy/gdpr/ (accessed August 2020).

[31] Moreover, the Budapest Convention of 2001 requires that member states ensure that many traditional offenses remain offenses when committed online (see footnote 33).

[32] One study in Azerbaijan found that passing information security (cybercrime) legislation "was a critical driver of increasing consumer confidence." Asian Development Bank (ADB). 2016. A Snapshot of E-Commerce in Central Asia. *Asian Development Blog.* 18 January. https://blogs.adb.org/blog/snapshot-e-commerce-central-asia.

[33] Council of Europe. 2001. *Convention on Cybercrime.* https://www.coe.int/en/web/conventions/full-list/-/conventions/rms/0900001680081561.

[34] For example, some legal systems do not traditionally recognize data as a form of property. Under existing laws, therefore, copying data without authority may not constitute theft, and deleting someone else's data may not constitute damage to property.

Azerbaijan and Georgia are the only CAREC countries that have become parties to the Budapest Convention of 2001. The main online offenses that convention signatories are required to prohibit are illegal access to information systems (computers and networks), illegal interception of computer communications, interference with data or systems, and the misuse of electronic devices. The offenses expressly include the creation and spread of malware that harms the ability to use one's computer and that may steal valuable information. This includes viruses, worms, ransomware, and the like.

A draft treaty prepared by the Russian Federation contains a list of offenses to be created by national law that is neither surprising nor particularly controversial and is in fact very similar to that of the Budapest Convention.[35] It also protects copyright "and related rights."[36] The real difference turns on enforcement. It gives more autonomy to states in their own investigations than does the Budapest Convention and requires less disclosure to and cooperation with other countries.[37] It does, however, have many provisions on cooperation, information sharing, extradition, and related powers.

CAREC countries understand that fighting cybercrime is exceedingly difficult. Cybercriminals take some pains to disguise their location and tend to attack indirectly. Consumer or user education is a crucial tool for resisting cybercrime. Making the target harder to attack is as important as fighting the attackers.[38]

Consumer Protection

When consumers are protected, they have greater trust and participate more in the economic system. Without such protection, they will stick mainly to familiar transactions with familiar people. There will be less economic activity, and much less of it will be online.

Consumer protection laws focus on the rights of people in respect of their purchases of goods and services for their personal or household use.[39] Some protections are best or generally provided by government regulation—notably, when public health and safety are involved. The interest of this study is on private rights when the sale is legal but there are problems with the transaction. It may be that the goods or services a consumer bought are not what was expected, or defective, or may cause harm (in a way not frequent enough to have the product banned).

Depending on a jurisdiction's civil justice system, consumer protection laws may involve regulatory supervision, private rights of action, or both. Key elements can govern the provision of information to the consumer—e.g., through labeling, notices in sales places, advertising restrictions—and the protection of the consumers' health and safety when they are unable to protect themselves. The Guidelines for Consumer Protection Legislation of the United Nations (UN), first developed in the 1980s, were updated in 2016 to cover online transactions and

---

[35]   Draft United Nations Convention on Cooperation in Combatting Information Crimes. https://www.rusemb.org.uk/fnapr/6394 (accessed August 2020).

[36]   The African Union Convention on Cybersecurity and Personal Data Protection (2014) takes the same approach and describes the offenses that member states must prohibit in their own laws. African Union. 2014. *African Union Convention on Cyber Security and Personal Data Protection.* https://au.int/sites/default/files/treaties/29560-treaty-0048_-_african_union_convention_on_cyber_security_and_personal_data_protection_e.pdf.

[37]   A. Peters. 2019. Russia and China are trying to set the U.N.'s Rules on Cybercrime. *Foreign Policy.* 16 September. https://foreignpolicy.com/2019/09/16/russia-and-china-are-trying-to-set-the-u-n-s-rules-on-cybercrime/.

[38]   The Government of Kazakhstan's cybersecurity page may be instructive and provide useful tips for the rest of CAREC countries, given that cyber criminality is worldwide (footnote 28).

[39]   Some jurisdictions protect small businesses or "mass market" purchasers, whatever the purpose of the purchase. These two groups purchase some of the same products, e.g., office furniture, computers, and software. The knowledge and bargaining power of small businesses making a purchase may be about the same as those of a consumer. The similarities between the groups can be dealt with by having general rules about honest sales, but remedies may differ for businesses.

modern practices, as well as environmental protection.[40] Azerbaijan states that its 2019 legislation in this domain follows these UN guidelines for consumer protection.[41]

Consumer protection laws worldwide tend to give the consumer the right to enforce the terms of the contract. Legislation may give consumers (and often merchants) special processes other than those provided by a standard civil court system to resolve disputes when they arise. The UN guidelines for consumer protection advocate "procedures that are expeditious, fair, transparent, inexpensive and accessible."[42] Depending on jurisdictions, several processes can be used either individually or in combination:

(i)   A government office, such as a consumer protection bureau, may have the authority to intervene in these disputes.[43]

(ii)   A special tribunal may exist or be established to settle consumer disputes or disputes below a certain value (e.g., small claims court). This tribunal may provide staff assistance or simplified procedures to help consumers pursue their claims.

(iii) A special legal process may be available that allows multiple consumers with similar small-value claims to combine them into a single legal action that is worth carrying forward (e.g., class-action suit).

(iv)   Mediation or arbitration processes may be funded by the government or permitted by law to facilitate resolution of disputes.

It may be possible to set up an online dispute resolution process for online sales. Some private models exist. They depend on both parties to a dispute opting to use them.[44] In some, extensive government support at the design and building stages is required.[45]

The remedies available from the merchant for a consumer who has been sold defective goods or services can vary between systems and include a refund of the purchase price, the replacement goods or services, cancellation of the payment obligation, and compensation for harm suffered. The state may choose to prosecute merchants who violate public standards of proper commercial conduct.

The UN guidelines for consumer protection say that member states "should provide or maintain adequate infrastructure to develop, implement and monitor consumer protection policies."[46] The educational function of consumer protection laws is widely acknowledged as a good in itself that provides the vulnerable with a measure of protection from exploitation.[47]

Online and offline sales differ in two main ways: in online sales, (i) the consumer generally does not see, examine, or test the physical goods before the sale; and (ii) the merchant may be remote from the buyer and sometimes in a different country. Legislation intended to apply to electronic commerce tries to compensate for these purchaser disadvantages. For example, it may (i) require merchants to disclose essential information and the sales contract itself in a timely way, and (ii) allow consumers a cooling-off period in which they can cancel the sale, (in some

---

[40]   UNCTAD. 2016. *United Nations Guidelines for Consumer Protection*. Geneva. https://unctad.org/en/PublicationsLibrary/ditccplpmisc2016d1_en.pdf. The guidelines are available in all official UN languages, notably Chinese and Russian. See also OECD.2016., Consumer Protection in E-commerce: OECD Recommendation, OECD Publishing, Paris. http://dx.doi.org/10.1787/9789264255258-en.

[41]   Government of Azerbaijan. 1995 (amended 2019). *Law of the Azerbaijan Republic about Consumer Protection*. Baku. https://cis-legislation.com/document.fwx?rgn=2795. The full text in Azeri is online: http://e-qanun.az/framework/9479 .

[42]   Footnote 40, Article 37, p. 15.

[43]   Specialist bureaus are another option. For example, the United States has a wide array of such bureaus for specific types of disputes, such as disputes involving trade, finance, broadcasting, and aviation.

[44]   See for example, Modria, a private online dispute resolution company that grew out of eBay's internal dispute resolution system that had handled millions of disputes. Tyler Technologies. Modria. https://www.tylertech.com/products/modria.

[45]   See, for example, the Civil Resolution Tribunal in British Columbia, Canada. British Columbia Civil Resolution Tribunal. https://civilresolutionbc.ca/.

[46]   Footnote 40, Article 8, p. 8.

[47]   The contents of a good educational program are described in the UN guidelines for consumer protection. Footnote 40, Article 44, p. 17.

cases also for cross-border transactions). The update of existing consumer protection rules in an EU directive from October 2019 focuses on online commerce.[48] Among other issues, the directive deals with free services (in exchange for personal information), mandatory contact information, explanation of rankings, and reviews.[49] CAREC countries planning to enact or update consumer protection laws may wish to consider these rules.

The UN guidelines for consumer protection pay special attention to the need for sustainability in development and in the use of consumer resources, as well as to the environmental impact of production for consumption. They underline the need for state support for and guarantee of the supply of food, water, pharmaceuticals, and energy, and the operation of public utilities. Consumer protection laws should be adequate to address the marketing and the provision of goods and services related to tourism, which is becoming a large part of economies and an important source of livelihood in a growing number of countries.[50]

Consumers are increasingly likely in the internet age to engage in cross-border commerce. An important phenomenon of global consumer commerce has been international cooperation between enforcement agencies to try to keep this trade honest. This cooperation is currently embodied by the International Consumer Protection and Enforcement Network, which was promoted by the UN guidelines for consumer protection.[51] Of its 62 member countries, 3 are CAREC countries: Azerbaijan, Mongolia, and the PRC.

In summary, consumer protection legislation is well worth having, but states must be careful not to build expectations that cannot be met. State actors must almost inevitably take part in making consumer protection measures work, both at the advice stage and in enforcement. While this may appear expensive, it is worth considering whether it will be even more costly to have consumers and businesses avoid the potentially dynamic e-commerce economy altogether because adequate protection is not being provided.

Other Areas of Regulation Affecting Electronic Commerce

The legal and regulatory framework for electronic commerce overlaps with many other areas of law: commercial and procedural, public, and private.

Electronic Payment

All commerce requires payment, and e-commerce works best with e-payments. For B2C transactions, the world standard is e-payment through credit cards. The card issuer takes the responsibility for identifying and authenticating the card holder and ensures that the merchant is paid (within some contractual limits).

Most CAREC countries allow the use of credit cards in most transactions. The terms of use are largely set by the large card organizations, notably Visa and Mastercard. Private nonbank providers of financial technology have recently begun to offer methods of payment as well, especially for consumer transactions. Alipay and Apple Pay are two of the better known, but a lot of platforms have been launched since, with digital payments gaining traction because of the coronavirus disease (COVID-19) pandemic. Legal systems will have to decide where this financial technology fits into their payment schemes. Central banks are likely to decide on what kinds of transactions these applications can be used for and what security they should provide. In the short run, however, the current limits on the amounts paid through these payment platforms may make the need for regulation less urgent.

---

[48]   EU. 2019. *Directive of the European Parliament and of the Council amending Council Directive 93/13/EEC and Directives 98/6/EC, 2005/29/EC and 2011/83/EU of the European Parliament and of the Council as regards the better enforcement and modernization of Union consumer protection rules.* https://data.consilium.europa.eu/doc/document/PE-83-2019-INIT/en/pdf.

[49]   A private law firm provided an overview of the new directive: Covington & Burling LLP. 2019. EU Adopts New Deal for Consumers. Inside Privacy. 13 November. https://www.insideprivacy.com/international/european-union/eu-adopts-new-deal-for-consumers/.

[50]   Footnote 40, Articles 69–78, pp. 22–24.

[51]   International Consumer Protection and Enforcement Network. https://www.icpen.org/.

In most CAREC countries, financial institutions rely on the relevant central bank to authorize and regulate electronic payments for commercial transactions. In some instances—Mongolia, for example—government agencies such as customs authorities that do a lot of these transactions set up accounts with their principal transactional partners. The partners may direct their banks to credit customs authorities electronically from accounts they keep funded for this purpose whenever amounts become due.

Electronic Evidence

E-transactions and e-payments produce electronic records. These will need to be presented to courts or other forums to resolve disputes and possibly to tax and customs authorities for their purposes. Local laws governing legal evidence need to make allowance for these electronic records.

UNCITRAL's Model Law on Electronic Commerce (MLEC) provides in Article 9 that electronic records are not to be denied admission in court proceedings solely because they are in electronic form.[52] They are to be given weight according to their reliability. That said, it is important to consider how vulnerable electronic records are to attack and modification, and to provide for some review of the records before legal decisions are based on them.[53]

Civil Liability

The law of civil liability helps to compensate people harmed by the faults of others. At the same time it may dissuade people—including businesses and manufacturers—from committing those faults in the first place. States designing the civil law framework of cross-border paperless trade must therefore examine who will participate in this trade, the relationships between the trading partners (buyers and sellers), what can go wrong, and who should bear the risk of this happening (i.e., who is best positioned to avoid the potential harm or best able to take out insurance against it). This is slightly complicated as many participants in a cross-border electronic trade system are public institutions—either government entities, such as customs services, or bodies performing public functions, such as inspection laboratories. Any limitation of legal liability in electronic cross-border trade should be disclosed before such trade begins to enable potential traders inside and outside a country to evaluate their risks. Such disclosure is well suited in the case of trading websites or government-sponsored facilities. The imposition of liability becomes more difficult with respect to legal persons outside the country, including exporters, importers, brokers, and state agencies in other countries where goods and services traded originate, are bound, or must transit. The risks of liability in trading could affect decisions to trade in a particular country.[54]

Most CAREC countries have a civil code that governs civil liability in the country. The general rule is the same in most countries: the person who causes harm by fault must compensate the person harmed. This rule could well apply to all participants in cross-border trade, subject to the following considerations:

(i)   Could businesses, notably insurers or anyone having to certify the existence of important facts, afford to bear the liability if their fault caused serious damage? The risk of liability could discourage anyone from undertaking such a business. One thinks in this regard of certification service providers (CSPs) in particular, which must attest to the identity of the creators of electronic digital signatures.

---

[52]   Footnote 18, Article 9.

[53]   This is considered in a model law on electronic evidence prepared privately by Stephen Mason, a British barrister. S. Mason. 2017. *A Convention on Electronic Evidence: helping to provide for certainty in international trade.* The full text of the draft available at https://www.researchgate.net/publication/309878298_Draft_Convention_on_Electronic_Evidence.

[54]   The study's discussion on civil liability draws heavily from Economic and Social Commission for Asia and the Pacific (ESCAP). 2019. Readiness Assessment for Cross-Border Paperless Trade: Mongolia. Bangkok (Box 4). https://www.unescap.org/sites/default/d8files/knowledge-products/MNG-CBPT%20readiness%20assessment%20report-FINAL%2B.pdf; and ESCAP. 2019. *Readiness Assessment for Cross-Border Paperless Trade: Uzbekistan.* Bangkok (Box 4). https://www.unescap.org/sites/default/d8files/knowledge-products/UZB-CBPT%20Readiness-FINAL%2B.pdf.

(ii)   States may need to consider the complexity of participation in an authentication system where multiple participants, private and public, are active. As with any technology, the operation of the system depends on the quality of hardware and software used, and thus on the reliability of their suppliers, as well as in many cases an operator bound by contract to a government ministry or agency.

Intellectual Property

Businesses trading into other countries will want to be confident that their intellectual property rights in the goods they ship will be preserved when they cross borders. The laws of most CAREC countries provide this protection, although there is little that is specific to e-commerce. Well-known and widely accepted methods exist to protect the different forms of intellectual property, notably copyrights, patents, and trademarks. CAREC countries are members of the World Intellectual Property Organization (WIPO) and adhere to most of its principal treaties.[55] Some CAREC countries also allow rights owners to apply electronically to register their rights in each country into which they are trading.

Dispute Resolution

The best legal rules in the world are of little use if they cannot be applied or made effective if contravened. A system of accessible independent courts is the ultimate enforcement method for legal rights. However, many business interests prefer private arbitration because proceedings can be private, expert arbitrators can be chosen rather than independently assigned, and procedures can to some extent be of their own design. Arbitration is particularly attractive in international disputes, because it means a party from one country is not forced to trust the neutrality of the courts of another. It is important that awards arising from international arbitration be enforceable in the country of the losing party. The New York Convention on the Recognition and Enforcement of Foreign Arbitral Awards provides for firm enforcement of such awards.[56] The UN Model Law on International Commercial Arbitration provides added confidence to its partners in cross-border trade.[57] Legislation following this model ensures that arbitrations on one country's territory will automatically be conducted in ways that should satisfy international trading partners. The model law's 2006 amendments contemplate the use of electronic agreements to arbitrate as well as arbitral awards in electronic form.

---

[55]   WIPO. WIPO Lex Database. WIPO-Administered Treaties. Contracting Parties: WIPO Convention. https://www.wipo.int/treaties/en/ShowResults.jsp?&treaty_id=1 (accessed 20 March 2021). An overview of the array of WIPO-related intellectual property rights can be found here: WIPO. WIPO Lex Database. WIPO-Administered Treaties. Summary Table of Membership of the WIPO and the Treaties Administered by WIPO, plus UPOV, WTO and UN. https://www.wipo.int/treaties/en/summary.jsp (accessed 20 March 2021).

[56]   New York Arbitration Convention. http://www.newyorkconvention.org/. All CAREC members except Turkmenistan have signed or acceded to the convention.

[57]   UNCITRAL. Status: UNCITRAL Model Law on International Commercial Arbitration (1985), with amendments as adopted in 2006. https://uncitral.un.org/en/texts/arbitration/modellaw/commercial_arbitration/status (accessed 21 March 2021). The model law is adopted in legislations of Azerbaijan, Georgia, Mongolia, and Turkmenistan.

4 International Influences on Electronic Commerce Readiness

A country with domestic laws that are friendly to electronic commerce has made a good start on e-commerce readiness, but two or more countries that have harmonized such laws and thus allowed their traders to know their rights and duties in each other's jurisdictions are doing even better. Bilateral, regional, and global agreements, conventions, treaties, and texts can resolve international e-commerce trade issues and sometimes domestic ones as well. A state's participation in such international agreements can provide the legal authority for electronic communications when its domestic laws do not yet do so. These agreements can have this effect either expressly or by providing rules that are media-neutral—i.e., rules that can be satisfied by electronic means at the option of the country that is a member state, or of parties from the member countries who are involved in private transactions.

Implementation by Central Asia Regional Economic Cooperation (CAREC) countries of such international treaties is worth considering. Many CAREC countries' laws provide that the nation's international treaties apply when such a treaty and national legislation are in conflict.[58] These multilateral and bilateral agreements can make e-commerce legally feasible for parties in participating states even when their domestic laws would otherwise restrict them. There are several existing international agreements that some CAREC member states might already be party to or might consider joining in the interest of legally enabling accelerated e-commerce growth.

Trade-Related Agreements Authorizing Electronic Communications

Several international trade-related treaties are open to electronic documents and communications. Few of these require the use of electronic documents, but a growing number authorize it. A country looking for legal authority to enable e-communications, especially in cross-border trade, may find it within its existing treaties or in agreements it may wish to join. The following examples are international agreements that some CAREC countries have already signed:

(i) **World Trade Organization Trade Facilitation Agreement.** Many provisions of the Trade Facilitation Agreement require members to provide paperless communications, including electronic payments.[59]

---

[58] The constitutions of some states provide that international agreements into which these countries enter are self-executing and obtain the force of law domestically as soon as they come into force internationally. Nevertheless, it has been suggested that such provisions cannot be relied on by themselves to give the full authority needed for e-communications in Uzbekistan, and this reasoning may be more widely applicable within CAREC. M. Stalbovskaya (update by M. Khasanov). 2019. Update: Legal Research in Uzbekistan. *GlobaLex.* http://www.nyulawglobal.org/globalex/Uzbekistan1.html.

[59] The World Trade Organization (WTO) Trade Facilitation Agreement is described here: WTO. Agreement on Trade Facilitation. https://www.wto.org/english/docs_e/legal_e/tfa-nov14_e.htm; and WTO. 2017. *Trade Facilitation Agreement fact sheet.* https://www.wto.org/english/tratop_e/tradfa_e/tfa_factsheet2017_e.pdf. All eight CAREC members that are WTO members have ratified the agreement.

The agreement provides for simplification, modernization, and harmonization of export and import processes. The best endeavor provisions of the agreement cover single and electronic windows.

(ii) **World Customs Organization's International Convention on the Simplification and Harmonization of Customs Procedures** (as amended, known as the "Revised Kyoto Convention"). The 2006 revision of the World Customs Organization (WCO) convention, which changed customs practice from inspecting every package to managing the risk of contraband and other unsuitable goods, promoted the use of electronic forms.[60]

(iii) **World Trade Organization's Agreement on the Application of Sanitary and Phytosanitary Measures.** The current versions of international sanitary and phytosanitary agreements allow or contemplate the exchange of information electronically. These include several treaties on the trade in plants, notably the International Plant Protection Convention from the Food and Agriculture Organization and the Agreement on the Application of Sanitary and Phytosanitary Measures that interacts with this convention.[61] In particular, the International Plant Protection Convention's international standards for phytosanitary measures provide guidance for the exchange of electronic phytosanitary certificates, and two CAREC countries are participating in a global initiative referred to as ePhyto Solutions.[62]

(iv) **United Nations Convention on the International Trade in Endangered Species.** The United Nations (UN) convention on trade in endangered species allows for electronic declarations of exemptions from trade bans using electronic forms.[63]

Electronic Commerce Provisions in Trade Agreements

International free trade agreements have in the past decade begun including provisions to harmonize the legal regimes governing e-commerce in the participating countries. This has not been incidental or merely for facilitation; instead, these agreements explicitly promote reforms to commercial law to frame the legal effect of e-commerce.

In some cases, the provisions aim only to bring the parties to a uniform level in their implementation of global standards. Such standards include the UN Commission on International Trade Law (UNCITRAL) model laws (footnotes 18 and 20). The provisions aim in other cases to compel parties to the trade agreements to adopt particular positions on controversial policies, such as a requirement that businesses locate data processing facilities in the country from which the data (particularly personal data) originate.

The phenomenon of pursuing paperless trade facilitation in recent international trade agreements was examined in 2017 by the Asian Development Bank (ADB) Institute focusing on electronic trade facilitation rather than on legal reforms that apply to private transactions.[64] Other papers, including from the World Trade Organization

---

60 WCO. 2008. *International Convention on the Simplification and Harmonization of Customs Procedures (as amended)*. Brussels. http://www.wcoomd. org/en/topics/facilitation/instrument-and-tools/conventions/pf_revised_kyoto_conv/kyoto_new.aspx. A guide to its provisions is here: WCO. 2006. *Revised Kyoto Convention: Your Questions Answered*. Brussels. https://www.wcoesarocb.org/wp-content/uploads/2018/07/1.-WCO-Revised-Kyoto-Convention.pdf.

61 WTO. The WTO and the International Plant Protection Convention (IPPC). https://www.wto.org/english/thewto_e/coher_e/wto_ippc_e.htm; and WTO. The WTO Agreement on the Application of Sanitary and Phytosanitary Measures (SPS Agreement). https://www.wto.org/english/tratop_e/sps_e/spsagr_e.htm.

62 Uzbekistan has initiated live exchanging in 2020 and the People's Republic of China (PRC) is one of the countries that pioneered the pilot-test of the ePhyto solutions in 2018. International Plant Protection Convention Secretariat. IPPC ePhyto Solutions. https://www.ephytoexchange.org/landing/ (accessed 20 March 2021).

63 Convention on International Trade in Endangered Species of Wild Fauna and Flora. 1973 (amended 1979 and 1983). Convention text. https://cites.org/eng/disc/text.php.

64 Y. Duval and K. Mengjing. 2017. Digital Trade Facilitation: Paperless Trade in Regional Trade Agreements. *ADB Institute Working Paper Series*. No. 747. Tokyo: ADB Institute. https://www.adb.org/sites/default/files/publication/321851/adbi-wp747.pdf.

(WTO) and the UN Economic and Social Commission for Asia and the Pacific (ESCAP), provide analysis of several agreements with e-commerce provisions.[65]

Given differing legal and cultural traditions of the parties involved, trade obligations are often at a high level or are aspirational, making it difficult to support commercially effective legislation or resolve practical implementation issues. For example, the Association of Southeast Asian Nations-Australia-New Zealand Free Trade Agreement signed in 2010 has a chapter on e-commerce.[66] The chapter provisions use language such as "the parties shall, where possible, endeavor to work towards…" and "shall encourage the interoperability of certificates…" to deal with the difficult question of the harmonization of the authentication systems on which mutual recognition of e-documents may depend.[67] These provisions state goals that the parties hope to somehow achieve one day but do not help to arrive at them.

Amid the heightened importance of digital trade and reinforced by the pandemic, trade agreements have emerged to be at the forefront of rule-making on digital trade issues. Notably, the Australia-Singapore Digital Economic Partnership Agreement, Digital Economy Partnership Agreement between Chile, New Zealand and Singapore and the Comprehensive and Progressive Trans-Pacific Partnership, aim to reduce trade barriers in digital economy, build comparative standards, and promote regulatory harmonization in domestic legal frameworks governing electronic transactions and cross-border business.[68]

Overall, if cross-border e-commerce is to deliver on its full potential, e-commerce issues must become an integral part of the trade policy agenda. There is an advantage to putting these provisions into trade agreements, since these agreements have a high public profile. These provisions can attract political attention in a way that technical law reform rarely does, which can generate the political will to implement them in domestic law.[69]

Trade-Related Agreements Silent on Paperless Communications

Ongoing participation by trading partners in international agreements—especially multilateral agreements—facilitate trade in general and also establish the groundwork for paperless trade. Building interoperability of border inspection and permission regimes—as well as trust in the trade practices of trading partners—provide a good base for the move to electronic communications.[70] For example, conventions that standardize the layout of trade

---

[65]   J. Monteiro and R. Teh. 2017. Provisions on Electronic Commerce in Regional Trade Agreements. *WTO Working Papers*. No. ERSD-2017-11. Geneva: WTO Economic Research and Statistics Division. https://www.wto.org/english/res_e/reser_e/ersd201711_e.pdf; G. Pasadilla. 2020. E-commerce provisions in RTAs: Implications for negotiations and capacity building. *Asia-Pacific Research and Training Network on Trade Working Papers*. No. 192. Bangkok: ESCAP. https://www.unescap.org/sites/default/files/AWP192%20Pasadilla%20Gloria_2.pdf; and J. Gregory. 2018. Trade Agreements to Promote E-Commerce II. *Slaw*. 8 November. http://www.slaw.ca/2018/11/08/trade-agreements-to-promote-electronic-commerce-ii/.

[66]   Association of Southeast Asian Nations-Australia-New Zealand Free Trade Agreement. Chapter 10. https://aanzfta.asean.org/index.php?page=chapter-10-electronic-commerce/.

[67]   Footnote 66, Articles 5(2) and (3). See also J. Gregory, 2019. Trade Agreements to Promote E-Commerce III. *Slaw*. 29 December. http://www.slaw.ca/2019/12/30/trade-agreements-to-promote-electronic-commerce-iii/.

[68]   World Economic Forum. 2020. Advancing Digital Trade in Asia. Community Paper. October 2020. Geneva. https://www.weforum.org/reports/advancing-digital-trade-in-asia.

[69]   The UN Economic Commission for Latin America and the Caribbean had this experience with Harmonization of ICT Policies and Legislation across the Caribbean, a multi-stakeholder project funded by the International Telecommunications Union to develop e-commerce law for Caribbean countries. After the project wound up, little progress was made on implementation. Projects are no substitute for political will. Economic Commission for Latin America and the Caribbean. 2015. Q&A: ECLAC participates in regional E-Commerce workshop. *The Hummingbird*. 2 (11). p. 7. https://repositorio.cepal.org/bitstream/handle/11362/41984/1/HummingbirdNovember2015.pdf.

[70]   These are largely trade agreements, not texts aiming at private law changes, but they can clear the way for private parties and government agencies to do business electronically.

documents or the description of goods in trade can help countries understand documents that arrive in foreign languages and may allow them to be set up for electronic processing even without translation.[71]

Some CAREC countries have already joined or are working toward joining some of these agreements or initiatives:

(i) **United Nations Convention on Contracts for the International Sale of Goods.** The agreement sometimes known as the Vienna Sales Convention sets basic rules for the sale of goods between parties in different states. It was adopted in 1980 and so does not deal expressly with e-commerce, but the UN Convention on Contracts for the International Sale of Goods Advisory Council, a private group of experts on sales law, has found the convention to be consistent with electronic communications and to operate in the same way when they are used.[72] This could have important consequences for countries that are parties to the convention (as are many CAREC members), since it applies automatically to international sales contracts unless the contracting parties opt out. In other words, the law mandatorily applicable to such contracts permits e-communications to make them. This could provide useful flexibility to businesses looking to do international sales with e-documents, especially in countries where international treaties prevail over domestic laws, which include most of the CAREC members.

(ii) **World Trade Organization.** The WTO sets the world's trade rules, and membership also qualifies a country to join the WTO Trade Facilitation Agreement (footnote 59). The WTO has had a program on e-commerce since 1998 but little actual law to show for it.[73] Some WTO members (not the organization itself) issued a joint statement calling for harmonized legal rules to govern international e-commerce.[74] Little progress has been made since although likely to intensity given growing focus on e-commerce and digital trade for economic recovery.[75]

(iii) **United Nations International Convention on the Harmonization of Frontier Controls of Goods.** This convention allows standard reference to products in trade, which makes standard forms and thus electronically readable documents easier.[76]

(iv) **United Nations Layout Key for Trade Documents.** The UN Layout Key is a document used in conjunction with the UN convention (footnote 76) to enable readers to understand forms even when the forms are prepared in a language that they do not comprehend.[77] The forms speak for themselves once they are standardized. The United Nations International Convention on the Harmonization of Frontier Controls of Goods makes the use of this layout mandatory for member states. The UN Centre for Trade Facilitation and Electronic Business (UN/CEFACT) says that the Layout Key "can also be used to design screen layouts for the visual display of electronic documents."[78]

---

[71] For example: UN Economic Commission for Europe. Trade Facilitation Implementation Guide. UN Layout Key. http://tfig.unece.org/contents/unlk-recomm-1.htm.

[72] UN Convention on Contracts for the International Sale of Goods-Advisory Council Opinion no. 1, Electronic Communications under CISG, 15 August 2003. http://www.cisgac.com/cisgac-opinion-no1/.

[73] Except an ongoing moratorium on customs duties on e-commerce transactions. WTO. Electronic commerce. https://www.wto.org/english/tratop_e/ecom_e/ecom_e.htm.

[74] WTO. 2019. DG Azevêdo meets ministers in Davos: discussions focus on reform; progress on e-commerce. News release. 25 January 2019. https://www.wto.org/english/news_e/news19_e/dgra_25jan19_e.htm.

[75] Y. Ismail. 2020. *E-commerce in the World Trade Organization: History and latest developments in the negotiations under the Joint Statement.* Negotiating brief prepared for the Geneva Seminar: Joint Statement Initiative on Electronic Commerce. Geneva. 29 January. https://www.iisd.org/system/files/publications/e-commerce-world-trade-organization-.pdf.

[76] United Nations Economic Commission for Europe (UNECE). 1982 (amended 2008 and 2011). International Convention on the Harmonization of Frontier Controls of Goods. http://tfig.unece.org/contents/Harmonized-frontier-controls-convention.htm. The full text is available at UNECE. 1982. *International Convention on the Harmonization of Frontier Controls of Goods.* Geneva. http://www.unece.org/fileadmin/DAM/trans/conventn/ECE-TRANS-55r2e.pdf.

[77] UN Centre for Trade Facilitation and Electronic Business (UN/CEFACT). Recommendation No. 1: UN Layout Key for Trade Documents. http://tfig.unece.org/contents/recommendation-1.htm.

[78] UNECE. Trade Facilitation Recommendations. Recommendation 1: UN Layout Key for Trade Documents. https://unece.org/trade/uncefact/tf_recommendations.

International Instruments and Institutions on Paperless Commerce

Several UN instruments and institutions provide guidance and support to member states in modernizing and harmonizing their legal systems to permit the use of electronic communications and electronic documents in international trade. These steps do not require the existence or establishment of international agreements. They are instead actions that individual countries can take on their own to make paperless trade easier. They often apply both at home and abroad, though sometimes only internationally. Either way, they build legal readiness for e-commerce.

United Nations Commission on International Trade Law

The principal international advocate of this harmonized modernization has been UNCITRAL. The organization's two principal model laws on electronic commerce are the Model Law on Electronic Commerce (MLEC) and the Model Law on Electronic Signatures (MLES) (footnotes 18 and 20). A third model law was adopted in 2017 that deals with electronic transferable records.[79] Providing the means to authorize electronic versions of transferable records such as bills of lading and warehouse receipts, it has been adopted by Bahrain and Singapore as well as UAE's Abu Dhabi Global Market as of July 2021.

UNCITRAL also created the UN Convention on the Use of Electronic Communications in International Contracts—generally shortened to the Electronic Communications Convention (ECC)—in 2005.[80] Among CAREC countries, Azerbaijan (effective 01 April 2019) and Mongolia (effective 1 July 2021) are contracting parties; while the PRC is a signatory to the ECC. Article 20, para 2 of the ECC provides a method by which a contracting state may interpret other international commercial conventions to which it is a party, in the light of UNCITRAL's e-commerce principles. This avoids the need to have these conventions modified expressly to allow e-communications. This could extend the benefits of such communications to many legal international relationships of CAREC member states. This is important to the CAREC member countries, where a good number of the current laws on electronic documents and signatures have yet to be fully in accordance with the UNCITRAL rules.[81] The UNCITRAL model laws on e-commerce and e-signatures (footnotes 18 and 20) are thus of moderate assistance at best in harmonizing the law of any CAREC member state with that of its trading partners to facilitate cross-border paperless trade. This should change. Of the four UNCITRAL instruments that touch on e-commerce, the ECC and accession to it should be made a CAREC country priority. This is especially true as the ECC restates much of the essence of UNCITRAL's first two model laws.[82]

United Nations Centre for Trade Facilitation and Electronic Business

UN/CEFACT has published numerous guidelines (called "recommendations") on various aspects of cross-border electronic communications.[83] The list of recommendations from UN/CEFACT, which includes aspects of electronic commerce, has been growing since the days of electronic data interchange in the 1980s. UN/CEFACT

---

[79] UNCITRAL. 2017. *UNCITRAL Model Law on Electronic Transferable Records.* Vienna. https://uncitral.un.org/en/texts/ecommerce/modellaw/electronic_transferable_records.

[80] UNCITRAL. United Nations Convention on the Use of Electronic Communications in International Contracts (New York, 2005). https://uncitral.un.org/en/texts/ecommerce/conventions/electronic_communications.

[81] All but one of the CAREC member countries have some form of electronic transaction legislation. Afghanistan has only a draft, which was circulated for discussion in 2016 but which has not been introduced as legislation.

[82] Several CAREC member states that are part of the former Soviet Union relaxed laws that had been originally influenced by the Russian Federation's older legislation, but others have not yet done so. The Russian Federation acceded to the ECC and made its law on e-signatures and e-documents more flexible in 2011.

[83] UN/CEFACT. https://www.unece.org/cefact/. The list of its recommendations is here: UNECE. Trade Facilitation Recommendations. https://unece.org/trade/uncefact/tf_recommendations.

has been particularly prolific since 2004 in supporting the construction and operation of single-window systems that focus cross-border shipping documents on a single point of entry or disposition in the interests of efficiency and consistency of treatment. Nonetheless, much earlier UN/CEFACT documents recommending a national coordinating body on international trade (Recommendation 4, originally published in 1974)[84] and on electronic signatures (Recommendation 14, made in 1979 and revised in 2014)[85] still provide good counsel. The more that CAREC members take inspiration from UN/CEFACT's recommendations, the better the chances are that their systems will work together smoothly.

United Nations Framework Agreement on Facilitation of Cross-Border Paperless Trade in Asia and the Pacific

In 2016, ESCAP adopted the Framework Agreement on Facilitation of Cross-Border Paperless Trade in Asia and the Pacific.[86] An official UN convention, the agreement has been adopted by five states, including two CAREC countries: Azerbaijan, which acceded in 2018 and the People's Republic of China (PRC), which ratified it in November 2020. The agreement came into force on 20 February 2021. The agreement sets out principles of a rational, acceptable, harmonized approach to cross-border paperless trade. It encourages parties to the agreement to create a national policy on this trade, establish a single window to handle documentation destined for different agencies within the state, and set up systems to promote the mutual recognition of trade documents among member states (and other trading partners). Each contracting party is to take these steps, which all align with international best practices, in ways consistent with its own legal system and traditions.

The framework agreement encourages rather than mandates, which allows ESCAP member states (including all the CAREC member countries) to join no matter how ready they currently are to engage in cross-border paperless trade. The rules serve as guides for those at the early stages, and as confirmation of steps already taken for those more advanced in the process. They provide a route along which all the parties can work in a consistent way (but at their own pace) to facilitate their trade with each other and the rest of the world. ESCAP may also be able to offer resources to help parties to the agreement engage in cross-border paperless trade.

United Nations Network of Experts for Paperless Trade in Asia and the Pacific

In addition to creating the Framework Agreement on Facilitation of Cross-Border Paperless Trade in Asia and the Pacific, ESCAP has published a great deal of advice on paperless trade and single windows. Worth noting is *Digital and Sustainable Trade Facilitation: Global Report 2019*.[87] This report gives countries context and understanding on what their neighbors are doing and their own strengths and weaknesses. It should be read in conjunction with subregional supplements, including the one covering CAREC countries.[88] It has done so mainly through the UN Network of Experts for Paperless Trade and Transport in Asia and the Pacific (UNNExT).[89] CAREC member states should take advantage of the regional expertise available through UNNExT to create or verify their own

84   UN/CEFACT Recommendation 4, National Trade Facilitation Bodies, New York and Geneva, 2015. https://unece.org/fileadmin/DAM/cefact/ recommendations/rec04/ECE_TRADE_425_CFRec4.pdf.

85   UN/CEFACT Revision of Recommendation 14, Authentication of Trade Documents, Geneva, 2014. https://unece.org/fileadmin/DAM/cefact/ recommendations/rec14/ECE_TRADE_C_CEFACT_2014_6E_Rec14.pdf

86   ESCAP. 2019. *Framework Agreement on Facilitation of Cross-Border Paperless Trade in Asia and the Pacific.* Bangkok. https://www.unescap.org/ resources/framework-agreement-facilitation-cross-border-paperless-trade-asia-and-pacific

87   UN. 2019. *Digital and Sustainable Trade Facilitation: Global Report* 2019. https://www.unescap.org/sites/default/d8files/knowledge products/ UNtfsurvey%20global%20report%202019.pdf.

88   While the UN prepared the global report, ESCAP separated the findings for particular regions. ESCAP. 2019. *Digital and Sustainable Trade Facilitation in Central Asia Regional Economic Cooperation.* https://www.unescap.org/sites/default/d8files/knowledge-products/UNTF%20 CAREC%20Report%20%282019.12.27%29.pdf.

89   A list of relevant studies and reports is available at UNNExT. Reports & Studies. https://unnext.unescap.org/reports-studies.

intellectual and policy frameworks for facilitating paperless trade and single windows, and to push these concepts further in collaboration with ESCAP members and UNNExT participants.

Mutual Recognition

A key dimension of mutual recognition is international trust and how to establish it—in practice, how to give legal effect in one country to electronic documents from another. Mutual recognition means reciprocal recognition: country A recognizes country B's e-documents, and B recognizes A's. That goal can be achieved by different legal mechanisms. Some will apply to particular types of transactions, e.g., shipping manifests for business-to-business (B2B) transactions, and customs forms for business-to-government ones. Others apply to particular kinds of documents or data, or possibly to authentication measures. Some mutual recognition methods require specific technology, while others support mutual recognition regardless of technology.

With respect to legal form, some mechanisms are treaty-based and may be self-executing and legally binding for that reason. Several CAREC countries' laws on electronic signatures say expressly that, if standards in an international treaty to which the country is a party contradict the rules set out in the statute, the treaty's provisions prevail.[90] Other countries may need to legislate for treaties to have a domestic effect. Some mechanisms favor harmonization of legal systems through the adoption of uniform laws. Still other mechanisms are based on memoranda of understanding and similar technical arrangements. Ideally, the temptation to specify one technology for international use should be resisted in favor of technology neutrality. One should not underestimate the complexity of comparisons even for concepts with similar labels. Technological specificity can be a barrier to innovation and efficiency.

The principles of the ESCAP framework agreement and UNCITRAL are important elements of an effective mutual recognition scheme. Harmonizing legal regimes is a good start but does not get countries all the way to mutual recognition. Likewise, the harmonization of forms of trade documents that often flows from membership in international agreements (including bilateral arrangements) is also very worthwhile. But reliable authentication is needed of the source and integrity of electronic documents to achieve mutual recognition under even such harmonized arrangements. A number of attempts have been made to solve this issue by harmonizing standards for digital signatures based on dual-key cryptography that represent the technology recognized by most CAREC member states. The focus of these efforts is often on the operations of the "trusted third party" needed to act as the certification service provider (CSP).[91]

Detailed comparison of the authentication policies and practices of different countries (known as "mapping" them against each other) takes a lot of work and involves a lot of difficult judgments. It must be established whether each concept and step on the side of one party has an equivalent on the other. Hardware, software, enrollment practices, and key certificate management must all be analyzed. It must then be determined whether the total of all the concepts and steps creates two systems with a similar level of reliability. Considerable efforts have been made to design cross-certification procedures for this purpose, with mixed success at best. The general requirements and trust of each country—or of each business within it—will depend on its own analysis and tolerance of the risks under given circumstances. Risks can be assessed differently for different activities. Moreover, mutual recognition must indeed be mutual. Whether certain A and B are individuals, trading partners, or public authorities, what A may confidently rely on, B may find unreliable. Judgments can also change, often

---

[90]   For example, the Law of Mongolia on Electronic Signatures, 2011, article 2.2, states, "If an international treaty to which Mongolia is a party is inconsistent with this law, then the provisions of the international treaty shall prevail." Ulaanbaatar. https://crc.gov.mn/en/k/2lq. Some qualifications apply, however.

[91]   The third party is one independent of both the signer and the person who wishes to rely on the signature. As shown in the country-by-country analysis in this study's Chapter V (Legislation of CAREC Countries), this function has a number of names.

depending on answers to the following questions: How much does one trust other states to adhere to the agreed standards? Are their governments and regulatory systems honest and competent? Supposing there is a change in government, do the certificates stay reliable?

It is arguable that cross-certification will work only where a consistent standard can be established and governed by one or more very trusted bodies. The closer a group of countries can come to adopting a common standard for authentication, the less they need to compare and evaluate one another's similar or not-quite-similar systems (policies and practices), and the more confident they can be in recognizing each other's signatures or (more likely) digital certificates. Achieving this common standard is difficult, however. For instance, the Eurasian Economic Union (EAEU), of which two CAREC countries are members and which a few other CAREC members are interested or negotiating to join, has been working on developing a "transboundary trust environment" at least since 2014. Finding common ground on these matters is hard even for similar and otherwise closely cooperating states.[92] UNCITRAL's Working Group on Electronic Commerce is currently exploring identity management and trust services.[93]

Ways forward. The many challenges involved in achieving mutual recognition could inspire some policy makers to consider using a simpler form of signature or even removing a signature requirement entirely. UN/CEFACT reviewed many alternatives to the use of signatures in its Recommendation 14, published first in 1979 and updated in 2014 to reflect current practices and technology.[94]

Rather than seeking an immediate global formula for mutual recognition that fully matches the rule of equivalent reliability in UNCITRAL's MLES, it may be possible to adopt mutual recognition incrementally or on a smaller scale with some adaptation, innovation, and flexibility, given the following:

(i)   Some countries (such as among the EAEU members) have expressed preferences for public sector government-to-government trusted communications in the early years of a new system. Such a limited system may be a workable avenue to explore. Governments may be able to exchange public signing keys directly with each other and thereby avoid dealing with technical questions (e.g., acceptance of common technical standards) about the practices of third-party certification authorities.

(ii)   Trust is seldom an all-or-nothing question. The strength of authentication required for any set of communications is open to discussion and amendment.[95] Trust management is a form of risk management.

---

[92]   EAEU. 2018. Outcome of the Supreme Eurasian Economic Council: programs aimed at forming common markets of gas, oil and petroleum products approved, Declaration on Further Development of Integration Processes within the EAEU signed. News release. 12 July. http://www.eurasiancommission.org/en/nae/news/Pages/07_12_2018_1.aspx. The programs include: Article 2 (part): creating the common digital business space based on harmonization of approaches and compatibility of technologies, in particular, developing cross-border space of trust, mutual recognition of legal importance of digital processes and services.

[93]   A first draft of a set of rules was considered at the meeting of the working group in November 2019. The reports of the working group and draft texts for discussion on this topic are available here: UNCITRAL. Working Group IV: Electronic Commerce. https://uncitral.un.org/en/working_groups/4/electronic_commerce.

[94]   The recommendation encourages states to reduce the instances where any kind of signature is required as much as possible, noting the desirability of other forms of authentication. Annex B.2 of Recommendation 14 lists a number of electronic alternatives to handwritten signatures, without stating any preference for particular purposes. UN/CEFACT. 2014. *Revision of Recommendation 14: Authentication of Trade Documents.* Geneva. https://www.unece.org/fileadmin/DAM/cefact/recommendations/rec14/ECE_TRADE_C_CEFACT_2014_6E_Rec14.pdf.

[95]   Annex B.1 of UN/CEFACT Recommendation 14 contains a long list of factors to consider in deciding what kind and degree of authentication may be wanted for different purposes. From this list one may draw at least two conclusions. First, a detailed mapping of one system against another can be very complex, since so many different goals are being sought by each system. Almost every user and certainly every industry and every country covered by such a mapping process will have its own view of the risks it is subject to, the risks it is willing to support, and the acceptability of somebody else's assurance of trustworthiness. The second and more optimistic conclusion is that there may be at least some elements of A's system that B may be comfortable accepting.

(iii)   Government-based authentication systems may be considered more trustworthy than private sector ones. If private parties rely on government-issued authentication, such as national identity cards, to obtain signature creation data, their certificated signatures can be more persuasive not only at home but in other countries.[96]

(iv)   Some CAREC countries already provide potential for achieving a degree of international mutual recognition in their e-commerce laws. For example, a law in Mongolia states the following: A "certificate according to relevant foreign legislation can be used in Mongolia."[97] A foreign (presumably closely related) CSP could be invited to harmonize its standards and practices with Mongolia's (or those of any other country with a similar provision), at least for certificates to be used in Mongolia. Mongolia's regulator would have to decide in an authoritative way that the foreign certificate was in practice issued in accordance with Mongolian law. This might be done without engaging in a full-scale cross-certification of a CSP's entire range of services.

(v)   Another option is the adoption of a rule in Azerbaijan's law regarding electronic signatures and electronic documents. This allows a foreign entity to apply for a certificate in the country of destination of the documents (and, perhaps, of goods or services).[98] If necessary, the operating documents themselves could be altered to suit the standards of their destination.[99]

[96]   For example, the electronic identification, authentication, and trust services regulation of the European Union (EU). https://ec.europa.eu/digital-single-market/en/policies/trust-services-and-eidentification.

[97]   Government of Mongolia. 2011. *Law of Mongolia on Electronic Signature*. Ulaanbaatar (Article 17.1). https://crc.gov.mn/en/k/2lq/1q.

[98]   Government of Azerbaijan. 2004. *Law of the Republic of Azerbaijan on Electronic Signature and Electronic Document*. Baku (Article 16). https://mincom.gov.az/upload/files/55d6592556a028f7d533d589f283c4c7.pdf.

[99]   Such a workaround would be feasible only when the volume of trade was sufficient to justify the reformatting, but that is also true of a mutual recognition scheme.

5 Legislation of CAREC Countries

The preceding chapters have outlined the challenges that electronic communications pose to legal relationships, and the main resources that the global community has available to meet these challenges. Central Asia Regional Economic Cooperation (CAREC) countries have varied in their use of these resources. This has depended to an important degree on the needs of their economies, but also on their legal traditions and what their neighbors were doing. As a result, their laws on e-commerce topics often both differ and share common elements. This chapter reviews mainly the primary legislation or principal legal texts of each CAREC country in the areas of electronic transactions, privacy, cybercrime, and consumer protection.[100]

The gaps between legal and actual implementation can make it difficult to find the best path forward. Implementing regulations are rarely available, although some reference is made in the statutes of several countries to subordinate (or other) legislation. In addition, little information has been available on what happened in practice once CAREC country legislation relevant to e-commerce was put in place, although the answer in some cases is, not as much as the breadth of the statutes seems to suggest. Part of this difficulty is because of other factors identified by the 2018 study by the Asian Development Bank (ADB) and the UN Economic Commission on Asia and the Pacific (ESCAP) as affecting e-commerce development: the degree of economic development and availability of the technology, plus the level of social and consumer trust in online transactions (footnote 5). Laws enacted may not lead to practical e-commerce development even where these are not barriers. For example, no party may be willing to take on the risks of acting as a certification service provider (CSP). A working and trusted program to accredit such businesses may not yet exist. Governments may not be willing or able to set up mechanisms to protect personal information or enforce consumer rights.

Anyone proposing to engage in law reform in CAREC countries needs to consider what is likely to happen in the marketplace as well as in the legislature. The appendix shows an overview of e-commerce related legislation in CAREC countries. The appendix does not make a judgment on the quality of the specific provisions or effectiveness of their implementation; instead, it only attempts to identify where potential areas of reforms could be made.[101]

---

[100] While attempts are made to refer to government-published laws, not all legislations are available online. Secondary sources were used for review purposes. The Commonwealth of Independent States, which includes some CAREC Program members, has a useful online database of its members' legislation, although it does not contain all the relevant texts. It offers all its texts in Russian, with machine translation into English. See Commonwealth of Independent States. Legislation of the CIS Countries database. https://cis-legislation.com/. Some internet browsers will also translate text they find in a language that is foreign to the reader. Where English text is not available, translation of documents reviewed are machine-based (artificial intelligence) and unofficial.

[101] Tables 9 and 10 provide recommendations for domestic law reforms and accession to or adoption of international instruments.

Afghanistan

Electronic transactions. Afghanistan is unique among CAREC member states in having no e-transactions legislation. An electronic transactions statute was introduced for consultation in 2015, but a copy of it was not available for this study. The best source of information on Afghanistan's readiness and potential for e-commerce is in the 2019 United Nations Conference on Trade and Development (UNCTAD) rapid e-trade readiness assessment.[102]

Privacy. Afghanistan does not have privacy legislation. While it may not be a priority, it should be on the long-term agenda in a form consistent with international best practices.

Cybercrime. Afghanistan has amended its Penal Code to add or consolidate provisions on cybercrime.[103] Among the crimes covered include the following:[104]

(i)   disrupting a computer network;

(ii)   using illegal means to access a computer system, programs, and computerized information;

(iii)   changing or destroying a computer system or the password and security code of the system;

(iv)   installing viruses in the system;

(v)   disclosing the password or security code of an information system;

(vi)   preventing others from having access to an information system;

(vii)   creating, preparing, and using an information system to commit crimes;

(viii) electronic counterfeiting and electronic fraud;

(ix)   theft of another person's internet service;

(x)   engaging in cyberterrorism or espionage; and

(xi)   producing or distributing child pornography.

These cybercrime provisions make up a comprehensive legal regime, consistent with the Budapest Convention of 2001 (footnote 33) and allow for policing internet use for the first time in Afghanistan. Observers have noted that the ability of police to investigate and lay charges remains to be demonstrated; some raised questions regarding the international aspects of cybercrime and the difficulties these may present to the use of digital evidence.[105]

Consumer protection. The Law on Consumer Protection was enacted in 2017.[106] A government web page sets out the main areas of protection as the rights to safety, to be informed, to consumer education, to choose, to be heard, to redress, to a healthy environment, and to satisfaction of basic needs.[107] These provisions can make for good consumer protection, if the law can become widely known and put into practice. Some of these rights are not private ones—i.e., enforceable against a transacting party—but instead public rights that are to be achieved through a political or social contract rather than a legal one.

---

[102]   UNCTAD. 2019. *Afghanistan Rapid eTrade Readiness Assessment*. Geneva. https://unctad.org/en/PublicationsLibrary/dtlstict2019d5_en.pdf

[103]   The full Penal Code in Pashto and Dari is available at Government of Afghanistan, Ministry of Justice. 2017. *Penal Code (in Pashto and Dari)*. Kabul. http://old.moj.gov.af/Content/files/OfficialGazette/01201/OG_01260.pdf.

[104]   Government of the United States, Library of Congress. 2017. Afghanistan: Cyber Crime Code Signed into Law. News release. 16 August. https://www.loc.gov/law/foreign-news/article/afghanistan-cyber-crime-code-signed-into-law/.

[105]   Afghanistan's Cyber Crime Law: A digital watchdog or another futile ambitious effort. Pajhwok Afghan News. 6 July 2017. https://www.pajhwok.com/en/opinions/afghanistan%E2%80%99s-cyber-crime-law-digital-watchdog-or-another-futile-ambitious-effort.

[106]   Government of Afghanistan, Ministry of Justice. 2016. *Law on Consumer Protection (in Pashto and Dari)*. Kabul. http://old.moj.gov.af/Content/files/OfficialGazette/01201/OG_01241.pdf.

[107]   Government of Afghanistan, Ministry of Industry and Commerce. Competition Promotion and Consumer Protection. https://moci.gov.af/en/competition-promotion-and-consumer-protection.

Azerbaijan

Electronic transactions. Azerbaijan has been a party to the United Nations (UN) Electronic Communications Convention (ECC) since 2019. Azerbaijan has a single e-transactions statute: the Law of the Republic of Azerbaijan on Electronic Signature and Electronic Document enacted in 2004 and amended in 2008 and 2016.[108] The statute is a hybrid, in that it allows for electronic signatures and documents not created by cryptography, as well as for those clearly within a public key infrastructure (PKI). An electronic document must be "confirmed" with an electronic signature. An electronic signature has no special technical characteristics, being "data added to or logically associated with other data to identify the owner of the signature," though not expressly to associate the owner of the signature with the document. An electronic signature "cannot be invalidated" for its electronic form or because it does not have a certificate.[109]

A basic signature and document can be used in a "corporate information system"—a system with "a limited number of users". Such a system may have its own internal regulation for e-documents and e-signatures. The definitions do not contemplate an open system of private contracting (buying and selling) by members of the public. Users of the basic signatures have to be bound by contract or common employment before the transaction arises.[110]

Certified signatures. Outside such a private system, an electronic signature has the same legal effect as a handwritten signature if it is "created by certified means" and has a "valid full certificate" which is one from an accredited certification service center (CSC). An electronic document with such a signature meets the legal conditions for submission of a document in writing. However, the law goes on to say that an electronic document—with no specification of the kind of signature it must bear "is equivalent to a document on paper and has the same legal force" unless the law requires notarization or state registration. An "enhanced" signature is one that is subject to close control by its owner.[111] The criteria for a reliable e-signature (footnote 108, Article 1.1.5) resemble (though appears to be more stringent than) those in the Model Law on Electronic Signatures (MLES) of the United Nations Commission on International Trade Law (UNCITRAL).[112]

Enhanced signatures may be certified by a CSC, which may or may not be accredited by the state. The "relevant state authority" does the accreditation and can issue a "full certificate," which has more legal power than other certificates. Communications among state authorities need to be done with enhanced and certified signatures, and in some cases only with accredited certificates. CSCs need a government permit to operate, whether they are accredited or not. The law sets out the responsibilities of a CSC to the owner of the signature and to parties who may rely on the certificate to identify the signatory to a document. It also prescribes the duty of the owner of the signature, for example, to keep the personal signing data confidential and to report to the CSC if the data may have been compromised. These responsibilities and the administrative structure of the PKIs are traditional, some of them echoing the MLES. The issuance of a certificate to the signatory requires the presentation of the owner's identity card. Each certificate has to be registered and bear information as provided by law to be included.[113]

Liability. CSCs are responsible for the completeness and accuracy of the certificates, and the quality and accuracy of their services. While the owner of the signature is liable for loss caused by not telling the CSC of a compromise to the system and is "responsible for protecting the information used to create a signature," there

---

[108]   Government of Azerbaijan. 2004. Law of the Republic of Azerbaijan on Electronic Signature and Electronic Document. Baku. https://mincom. gov.az/upload/files/55d6592556a028f7d533d589f283c4c7.pdf. See also Law of the Azerbaijan Republic about the Digital Signature and the Electronic Document (2004, amended 2008, 2016): Baku. http://cis-legislation.com/document.fwx?rgn=7428.

[109]   Footnote 108, Articles 1.1.15, 1.1.4, and 3.1.

[110]   Footnote 108, Articles 1.1.24, 7, and 26.4.

[111]   Footnote 108, Articles 1.1.12, 3.2 through 3.5.

[112]   Footnote 20.

[113]   Footnote 108, Articles 1.1.13 through 1.1.14, 6.1 through 6.4, 9, 11.2, 11.5, and 12.

is no express liability for having failed in this task including unauthorized access by someone who then commits fraud by using the signature.[114]

Routine matters. The Azerbaijan law has some provisions that are largely consistent with UNCITRAL's Model Law on Electronic Commerce (MLEC) (footnote 18), such as the rules on date and place of transmission and receipt of messages. Nothing speaks directly to questions of electronic evidence, though it is arguable that saying that an electronic document has the same legal value as one on paper could help get it admitted in evidence.

Foreign certificates. The Azerbaijan law addresses foreign certificates in two ways. First, it recognizes a foreign certificate that meets Azerbaijan's standards, either by direct proof, by its issue by a foreign certification center that has been accredited by Azerbaijan, or by its being covered by a guarantee by an Azerbaijan CSC.[115] The Azerbaijan CSC is liable under this guarantee for any losses suffered by the owner of the signature—but not, apparently, for losses by the party who relied on the signature and would seem to bear the greater risk. Second, the law recognizes a certificate "issued by the centers provided for in interstate agreements recognized by the Republic of Azerbaijan". It is not clear whether any such agreements exist or, if they do, what standards they apply.[116] In 2017, a decree authorized the issuance of digital signature certificates to foreigners and Azerbaijanis living abroad for their use in communications and documents crossing the borders of Azerbaijan.[117] Certificates need the signatory's mobile phone and subscriber identity module card for authentication.

Privacy. The Law on Personal Data was enacted in 2010.[118] It establishes a standard and reputable set of rules to protect individuals' privacy. Personal data expressly include biometric information, defined (properly) to include handwriting and signatures. Data may be collected only for specified purposes, and the law does not provide for any change of these purposes. If the purpose is satisfied, the data must be destroyed. There is a national register of databases of personal data. Personal data, once collected, must be held securely, but access must be provided to the data subjects to give them a right to correction and to require destruction of their data (the equivalent of revoking their consent to collect it).[119] The law applies to private and public sector collection and use of personal data. The relevant organ of executive authority oversees compliance with the statute.[120] Azerbaijan is a party to the Council of Europe's 1981 Convention for the Protection of Individuals with Regard to Automated Processing of Personal Data.[121]

Cross-border transfer of personal data. The Law on Personal Data prohibits the cross-border transfer of personal data unless the legislation of the destination country gives protection "at the level established" by Azerbaijan law, the data subject consents to the transfer, or consent is not needed domestically (for protection of the life or health of the subject).[122]

Cybercrime. Azerbaijan is a member of the Budapest Convention of 2001.[123] In compliance with it, the country prohibits certain activities concerning computers in its criminal code and in ways that are similar to those in effect in most CAREC countries. The Criminal Code of the Republic of Azerbaijan provides that unauthorized access to

---

[114]   Footnote 108, Articles 17 and 20.
[115]   Footnote 108, Articles 16.01 through 16.03. The "relevant executive authority" of the Republic of Azerbaijan carries out the accreditation of domestic and foreign centers and publishes a list (Footnote 108, Articles 33.2.8 and 33.2.10).
[116]   Footnote 108, Articles 16.02.4 and 17.6.
[117]   Government of Azerbaijan. 2017. *On Approval of Rules for Issuance of Electronic Signatures Certificates to Non-Residents through Diplomatic Missions and Consulates of the Republic of Azerbaijan.* Baku. http://e-qanun.az/framework/36462 (in Azerbaijani).
[118]   Government of Azerbaijan. 2010 (amended 2018). *Law of the Azerbaijan Republic about Personal Data.* Baku. http://cis-legislation.com/document.fwx?rgn=31412.
[119]   Footnote 117, Articles 5.9, 7, 9.1, 9.4, 9.5, 9.8, 10.1, 11.1, and 15.
[120]   Footnote 117, Article 17.
[121]   Footnote 26.
[122]   Footnote 117, Articles 14.2.2 and 14.3.
[123]   Footnote 33.

"law-protected computer information" is prohibited if damage is caused.[124] Just looking around without stealing (copying or downloading) data does not seem to be covered. A higher penalty is imposed if the crime is done by a group or by an official using his official position or if committed against a computer that is part of important public infrastructure. Spreading malware is contrary to law.[125]

Consumer protection. Consumer protection is provided in Azerbaijan largely through the Law about Electronic Commerce, enacted in 2005 and amended in 2016 and 2018.[126] Other civil laws may also apply. The basic rules include full disclosure by merchants of their identity and location and of information about the goods or services to be sold. Merchants may be civilly liable for misrepresentation. Disclosure has to be comprehensible to the non-expert buyer and some information needs to be given to prospective buyers before the sale or on conclusion of the contract. If this does not occur, the buyer can cancel the contract within 7 working days, at which point the seller must refund any part of the price paid. The law sets out rights and responsibilities for online intermediaries as well. Most of the provisions excuse intermediaries from defects in communication for which they are not in practice responsible. The law also allows for online dispute resolution if desired.[127]

People's Republic of China

Electronic transactions. The People's Republic of China (PRC) has two main statutes relevant to electronic transactions. The first, Electronic Signature Law of the People's Republic of China, is a fairly standard hybrid statute, with a number of provisions drawn from or influenced by the MLEC (footnote 18), along with provisions about certificates for digital signatures.[128] In brief, it deals largely with matters of authentication. The second, the E-Commerce Law of the People's Republic of China, tends to have more commercial provisions and is effectively an online supplement to other commercial laws.[129] Both were recently amended and the E-Commerce Law came into force on 1 January 2019.

The Electronic Signature Law defines an electronic signature as data in an electronic message attached to the identity of the signatory and indicating that the signatory approves the content. This is very close to the MLEC's rule, aside from the appropriate reliability test. Transacting parties may agree to use or not to use e-communications. The law also echoes the nondiscrimination clause of the MLEC.[130] There is case law in the PRC validating the use of a simple electronic signature, for example in an e-mail. A number of provisions in the law essentially follow the content and the order of the MLES (footnote 20). "Reliable" signatures are defined in terms of the MLES. The law does not say expressly when one needs to use a reliable e-signature rather than an ordinary e-signature. It goes on to provide for certificates for e-signatures, starting with the qualifications of an electronic CSP. Some of these also reflect the MLES, such as the requirement for appropriate personnel. The PRC has added others, such as the need for consent from the national password management agency.[131] A CSP must be registered with the government. Administrative details are set out, along with the contents of the certificate, which are standard provisions.

---

[124] Government of Azerbaijan. 1999. *Criminal Code of Azerbaijan*. Baku (Articles 271 - 273). Baku. https://www.legislationline.org/download/id/8304/file/Azerbaijan_CC_am2018_en.pdf.

[125] Footnote 124, Article 272.

[126] Government of Azerbaijan. 2005 (amended 2018). *Law of the Azerbaijan Republic about Electronic Commerce (Trading)*. Baku. http://cis-legislation.com/document.fwx?rgn=9111. This site refers to it as the law about "electronic trading," but "electronic commerce" is probably more accurate. http://e-qanun.az/framework/10406 (in Azerbaijani).

[127] Footnote 126, Articles 5, 7.3, 8, 9.1, 9.3, 11.2, 12, and 13.1.

[128] Government of the PRC. 2019. *Electronic Signature Law of the People's Republic of China*. Beijing. http://pkulaw.cn/fulltext_form.aspx?Gid=331476&Db=chl (in Chinese).

[129] Government of the PRC. 2018. *E-Commerce Law of the People's Republic of China*. Beijing. http://pkulaw.cn/fulltext_form.aspx?Gid=321035&Db=chl (in Chinese).

[130] Footnote 128, Articles 2 and 3.

[131] Footnote 128, Articles 2, 6, and 17.

Under the liability rules, the signatory has to disclose any breach of security. If it does not, or is not truthful in disclosures, the signatory is then liable for losses to the relying party and CSP. If the signatory or relying party suffers a loss because of the actions of the CSP, the CSP will be liable to compensate them unless it can prove that it was not at fault. Anyone committing fraud in the use of a signature is civilly and criminally liable for losses caused.[132]

Foreign certificates. A certificate issued by a foreign CSP has the same legal effect as a certificate issued by a CSP within the PRC if it has been approved by the government regulator "in accordance with the relevant agreement or the principle of reciprocity" (footnote 128, Article 26). The "principle of reciprocity" seems to refer to some formal arrangement to reciprocate that requires confidence in each CSP's practices. It is not clear that any such agreement exists, or where any such reciprocity operates.

Privacy. The protection of personal privacy in the PRC is a long-term project that is not yet complete. The principal statute at present is the Cyber Security Law of 2017.[133] Two legislative milestones are being considered by the National People's Congress: one on the Personal Information Protection Law and second on the Data Security Law.[134] The E-Commerce Law (footnote 129) provides that e-commerce operators who collect and use personal information must abide by law and administrative regulations on its protection—which would mean the Cyber Security Law and the related instruments. The E-Commerce Law also gives people a right to have their personal information corrected or deleted by the holders.[135]

The Cyber Security Law is much like good privacy laws in CAREC and elsewhere. The PRC's Cyber Security Administration regulates compliance generally. It is not clear, however, that any of these rules apply to the government itself as it collects information on individuals for various purposes.

Cybercrime. The Criminal Law of the PRC has several articles on crime relating to computers or their contents.[136] Unauthorized access to computers storing specific kinds of content, such as state secrets are prohibited. Violation of state regulations on deletion, alteration, addition, or interference in computer information systems with grave consequences, and spread of computer virus, malware or other programs are penalized.[137]

Consumer protection. The PRC enacted the Consumer Rights Protection Law of the People's Republic of China in 2013.[138] The E-Commerce Law also has a number of provisions on good, honest business practice that could be considered consumer protection.[139] The Consumer Rights Protection Law (footnote 138) does not say much about online sales and is mostly media neutral. Its provisions regarding product liability or banning misrepresentation could apply to e-commerce. The purchaser in online sales has an absolute right to return the goods for a refund within 7 business days—with the exception of purchases where that would not be fair to the seller (e.g., transactions involving perishables and consumables). An online trading platform may be liable

---

[132]   Footnote 128, Articles 27, 28, and 32. Article 28 has the potential to be very costly to CSPs. The statute does not mention any ability of the CSP to disclaim or limit liability by contract. In any case, there normally is no contract between the CSP and the relying party. This potential liability has affected the development of signature certification programs in many countries.

[133]   Government of the PRC. 2017. *Cybersecurity Law of the People's Republic of China. Beijing.* http://www.npc.gov.cn/ (in Chinese).

[134]   In October 2020, the PRC released the first draft of Personal Information Protection Law and Data Security Law. In April 2021, the second drafts of the proposed legislations were released for comments. http://www.npc.gov.cn/ (in Chinese). The draft Personal Information Protection Law aims to provide greater protections for personal information and create a data privacy regime that is more in line with the General Data Protection Regulation of the EU (footnote 27). Meanwhile, the draft Data Security Law is likely to provide for tightened restrictions on data export to overseas law agencies by imposing penalties for violation. Such restrictions may have an impact on the ability, or the willingness, of foreign businesses to trade with the PRC, especially if they need to comply with competing regulations at home.

[135]   Footnote 129, Article 24.

[136]   Government of the PRC. 1980 (as amended 1997). Criminal Law of the People's Republic of China. https://www.fmprc.gov.cn/ce/cgvienna/eng/dbtyw/jdwt/crimelaw/.

[137]   Footnote 136, Articles 285 and 286.

[138]   Government of the PRC. 2013. *Law of the People's Republic of China on the Protection of Consumer Rights and Interests.* http://pkulaw.cn/fulltext_form.aspx?Gid=211792 (in Chinese).

[139]   Footnote 129, Articles 5, 13, 15 through 17, 20, and 21.

to the consumer for harm as well if it cannot provide the name and contact information of the seller. If the platform does have to pay, though, it may recover its payout from the seller. The law also contains an array of administrative penalties against bad behavior toward consumers. State bodies are expected to punish the illegal and criminal acts of operators that infringe on the legitimate rights and interest of consumers. The law also requires a collector of personal information to disclose the purpose of the collection and to keep the information confidential.[140]

Summary. The PRC's legislations have been greatly modernized since the first version of the Electronic Signature Law in 2004 and responds to e-commerce well. With respect to electronic transactions, it is still hard to know when simple e-signatures and e-documents will work. This part of current legislation may need to be expanded. The certification process seems straightforward. There may be a question in practice about how liability would be allocated among market participants and affect their behavior. Other areas of the law are in the international mainstream. Privacy law is still a work in progress. The Consumer Protection Law appears to be largely in compliance with UN and Organisation for Economic Co-operation and Development (OECD) guidelines (footnote 40).

Georgia

Electronic transactions. Georgia's Law on Electronic Documents and Electronic Trust Services of 2017 is a hybrid statute.[141] It leaves room for simple electronic signatures to have some legal effect, while establishing and favoring a certificated digital signature regime for many purposes. The statute describes an "advanced electronic signature," which is essentially one with the characteristics of a reliable signature under the MLES (footnote 20): it is exclusively linked to the signatory and under the control of the signatory, and attached to the signed data so that any change to the data is detectable.[142] It also provides for a "qualified electronic signature," which is an advanced e-signature that is certified by a qualified trust services provider. Such a system resembles that of the European Union (EU).[143]

A qualified trust services provider is one that is accredited by a state agency (the Data Exchange Agency within the Ministry of Justice) applying criteria set out in the statute. CSPs must obtain civil liability insurance. CSPs are liable for "any damage resulting from a failure to fulfill obligations in accordance with this Law."[144]

Qualified trust services providers offer a qualified certificate to link the electronic digital signature with the public key of the signatory. The statute sets out the characteristics of such certificates, and also qualified time stamps as additional evidence of the validity of the certificates.[145]

A digital signature with a qualified certificate on an e-document has the same legal status as a handwritten signature on paper. Likewise, the integrity and original of an electronic document with a qualified electronic seal is presumed in the absence of evidence to the contrary.[146] Likewise, electronic documents may be used any time to satisfy a writing requirement.

---

[140] Footnote 138, Articles 25, 34, and 44.
[141] Government of Georgia. 2017. *Law of Georgia on Electronic Documents and Electronic Trust Services*. Tbilisi. https://matsne.gov.ge/en/document/view/3654557?publication=0.
[142] Footnote 141, Article 1(k).
[143] While the EU sets out detailed technical requirements for a signature to be qualified, Georgia's statute leaves such matters to regulations (Footnote 141, Article 2).
[144] Footnote 141, Articles 5, 5(2)(g), 5(4), and 11.
[145] Footnote 141, Articles 6 and 7.
[146] Footnote 141, Articles 3(1), 3(2), and 4(2).

Signed e-communications with public authorities have to use qualified e-signatures and administrative bodies must use them.[147] However, private parties—individuals or businesses—may agree that any electronic signature or electronic document for these individuals or entities shall have legal effect equivalent to a handwritten signature or a tangible document. The law allows private interests to use e-documents and e-signatures made according to "conventions" different from the law with the same legal effect.[148]

Foreign certificates. Qualified trust services under foreign law are recognized in Georgia if there is an international agreement to that effect.[149]

Privacy. Privacy is governed by the Law on Personal Data Protection enacted in 2011 and as updated.[150] As with most privacy statutes, its basic rule is that data should not be collected without the consent of the subject.[151] Georgia has a long list of exceptions to this rule. In 2014, Georgia reached a deep and comprehensive free trade agreement with the EU, by which it agreed to adopt the EU's privacy laws in a set of rules from 2002, but not the full General Data Protection Regulation (GDPR).[152] The text of the law has many of the features commonly found in CAREC countries' legislation.

A "personal data protection inspector" is charged with enforcing the rules. Anyone collecting data (referred to as a "data controller") in a way covered by the statute must register the collection with this inspector. A legal entity under private law and natural persons collecting biometric information need to disclose the fact to the inspector. The status and powers of the inspector are spelled out at some length, including enforcement powers and penalties. Direct marketers may use publicly available personal information to contact potential buyers, but people have the right to opt out of the marketing on request.[153]

Cross-border transfer of personal data. Personal information that is legally collected in Georgia may be transferred abroad if it is adequately protected in the destination country. If not, a transfer may occur if allowed by treaty. Private agreements between the Georgia data processor and the foreign state (or some other person or international entity there) on the protection to be granted need the approval of the personal data protection inspector. The inspector will evaluate whether the foreign country's protection is adequate by Georgia's standards.[154]

Cybercrime. Georgia is a member of the Budapest Convention of 2001 (footnote 33). The Criminal Code of Georgia prohibits the same offenses that most of the other CAREC member states do and use very close to the same language.[155] Unauthorized access to computers, the distribution of malware, and harm caused to computers and networks by someone who had access will be liable to computer-based penalties as the loss of activity privileges. Prison terms are possible if serious harm is done. In addition, it is an offense against the criminal code

---

[147]   Footnote 141, Articles 3(3).
[148]   Footnote 141, Articles 1(2) and 3(8).
[149]   Footnote 141, Articles 12.
[150]   Government of Georgia. 2016. *Law of Georgia on Personal Data Protection*. Tbilisi. https://matsne.gov.ge/en/document/view/1561437?publication=9.
[151]   Footnote 150, Article 5 (a).
[152]   The " Deep and Comprehensive Free Trade Agreement", officially Association Agreement between the European Union and the European Atomic Energy Community and their Member States, of the one part, and Georgia, of the other part, Brussels 2014. https://eur-lex.europa.eu/legal-content/EN/TXT/?uri=CELEX:02014A0830(02)-20180601. Annex XV-B requires Georgia within three years of the entry into force of the Agreement, thus by 2019, to bring its legislation into conformity with specified provisions of Directive 2002/21/EC of the European Parliament and of the Council of 7 March 2002 on a common regulatory framework for electronic communications networks and services (Framework Directive) as amended by Directive 2009/140/EC.
[153]   Footnote 150, Articles 8, 10, 20, 27 through 40, 43 through 54.
[154]   Footnote 150, Articles 41 and 44.
[155]   Government of Georgia. 1999. *Criminal Code of Georgia*. Tbilisi. https://matsne.gov.ge/en/document/view/16426?impose=translateEn&publication=209. Articles 284–286.

(footnote 155, Articles 341 through 362) and the Law on Electronic Documents and Electronic Signatures to forge a digital signature.[156]

Consumer protection. There appears to be no law specifically directed at protecting online or offline consumers, although standard prohibitions against fraud, forgery, and misrepresentation would apply to consumer transactions (for example, the Criminal Code of Georgia prohibits "cheating on consumers").[157]

Kazakhstan

Electronic transactions. Kazakhstan has adopted in 2003 the Law about the Electronic Document and Electronic Digital Signature following a Russian Federation model electronic transactions law, and has amended it to add flexibility.[158] An electronic digital signature validates the electronic document by providing evidence of integrity as well as origin. An e-document so validated is given the legal value of a signed paper document, and refusal to accept such a document is not allowed.[159] An electronic digital signature is given the same legal weight as a handwritten signature on paper if it is verified by a public key authenticated by a registration certificate issued by the accredited certification center that also created the signature.[160] State officials may use electronic digital signatures in certifying electronic documents for state purposes. For nongovernmental purposes, an electronic digital signature is used in the manner prescribed by the civil legislation of the Republic of Kazakhstan.[161] Such signatures may still need to be full dual-key cryptography signatures, rather than simpler form of electronic signature that parties to private transactions may choose. In short, the statute is still a technology-specific law.

The characteristics of the registration certificate (what other systems refer to simply as a certificate) include its issue by a certification center accredited by the government. The duties of the parties—the owner of the signature and the certification center—are elaborated in fairly standard terms for this kind of provision.[162] The statute also contains some procedural provisions about the management of e-documents, such as rules similar to those in the MLEC (footnote 18) about the time of sending and receipt of an electronic document.[163]

Foreign signatures and certificates. The law provides that a foreign electronic signature is the equivalent of a handwritten one in Kazakhstan if the signature has been issued and certified by a foreign certification center registered as a trusted third party of the Republic of Kazakhstan. A trusted third party is an entity that operates in cross-border matters to establish that a foreign signature or certificate is the equivalent of one created in Kazakhstan.[164] The statute sets out the rules for recognition of a signature based on a treaty, or one issued by a foreign certification center that has been recognized and registered by Kazakhstan's trusted third party, or one issued where the foreign trusted third party has itself been recognized and registered by its Kazakhstan equivalent. A parallel provision deals with the recognition of a foreign registration certificate. The "authorized body in the field of informatization" makes those determinations.[165] The statute does not say what the criteria

---

[156] Footnote 141, Article 17(2).

[157] Footnote 155, Article 219.

[158] Government of Kazakhstan. 2003 (amended 2020). *Law of the Republic of Kazakhstan about the Electronic Document and Electronic Digital Signature.* Nur-Sultan. http://cis-legislation.com/document.fwx?rgn=3148.

[159] Footnote 158, Article 24(2).

[160] Footnote 158, Article 10.

[161] Footnote 158, Articles 12(1) and 12(2).

[162] The translation of the statute seems to use the terms "certification authority" and "certification center" interchangeably. For example, Footnote 158, Article 20 translates its two provisions using "authority" the first time and "center" the second, but the Russian word used ("tsentr") is the same in each case.

[163] Footnote 158, Articles 7(2 through 4), 8 and 20(2).

[164] Footnote 158, Article 10(1-4). One reads the final "and" of the definition of "trusted third party" in Article 1(5-4) to mean "by comparison with," so that the foreign party must conform the Kazakhstan's standards of authentication practice in order to be a trusted third party.

[165] Footnote 158, Articles 1(1), 5(1-9), 13, and 19.

for a treaty or such recognition and registration would be. Nor does it state whether any such treaty exists, or whether any such recognition and registration occur regularly.

Privacy. Kazakhstan enacted privacy legislation in 2013, which was amended in 2020. The Law of the Republic of Kazakhstan about Personal Data and their Protection depends on the consent of the data subject for the collection, use, and disclosure of his or her personal data.[166] The statute contains many of the usual provisions of such legislation. The government use of personal information is governed by the Law of the Republic of Kazakhstan about Informatization.[167] The government has said that it plans to follow the principles of the EU's GDPR in its administration of its legislation. "On the basis of the general regulation, Data Protection Agency will operate in Kazakhstan" (footnote 28). The expected result of this policy is said to be making it more attractive for citizens and business to engage in digital trade in the country.

Cross-border transfer of personal data. The transfer of personal data to the territory of foreign states can generally be done only if the data will have similar protection there.[168] Transfers can be done to states that do not provide equal protection when the data subject consents; international treaties authorize it; it is necessary for health, morality, or public order; or it is necessary for protection of constitutional rights if consent is not available. These exceptions resemble those in force in some other CAREC members. Nonetheless, the free flow of personal data would be facilitated if similar degrees of protection were provided by neighboring states.

Cybercrime. Article 227 of the Criminal Code of the Republic of Kazakhstan establishes many of the usual offenses relating to computers. Unauthorized access to a computer resulting in erasing, blocking, modifying, copying, or disturbing work is an offense. The offense is aggravated if done by a group or by persons abusing their official position. Spreading malware has more severe penalties if the consequences are grave.[169]

Consumer protection. Kazakhstan has a thorough and well-thought-out Law of the Republic of Kazakhstan about Consumer Protection, enacted in 2010 and amended in 2020.[170] It gives consumers express rights to information and safe products and services, restricts the ability of suppliers to limit those rights, and provides for state and private enforcement. Most of its provisions are media neutral, but an article on online trading platforms ensures that these will operate fairly as well.[171]

In addition, standard prohibitions against fraud, forgery, and misrepresentation would apply to consumer transactions. The Regulation of Trading Activities Law of 2004, which has applied to e-commerce at least since 2015, makes the equal protection of the rights and legitimate interests of consumers a "principle of trading".[172] The regulation governs the disclosure of terms of e-commerce transactions, for consumers and others, as well as the duties of intermediaries.[173]

---

[166] Government of Kazakhstan. 2013 (amended 2020). *Law of the Republic of Kazakhstan about Personal Data and their Protection*. Nur-Sultan. http://cis-legislation.com/document.fwx?rgn=59981. Article 7.

[167] Government of Kazakhstan. 2015 (amended 2020). *Law of the Republic of Kazakhstan about Informatization*. Nur-Sultan. http://cis-legislation.com/document.fwx?rgn=80847.

[168] Footnote 166, Article 16. This interpretation extrapolates from the translation, "the transfer ... is performed only in case of ensuring personal data protection with these states."

[169] Government of Kazakhstan. 1997. *Law of the Republic of Kazakhstan No. 168 on Introduction of the Criminal Code of the Republic of Kazakhstan*. https://adilet.zan.kz/eng/docs/K970000167.

[170] Law about Consumer Protection, https://cis-legislation.com/document.fwx?rgn=31140.

[171] Footnote 169, Article 33 (1).

[172] Government of Kazakhstan. 2004 (as amended). *On the Regulation of Trading Activities*. Nur-Sultan. http://adilet.zan.kz/eng/docs/Z04000544_1. Article 3(8).

[173] Footnote 172, Article 29.1.

Kyrgyz Republic

Electronic transactions. The Kyrgyz Republic has gone further than other CAREC countries in updating its electronic transactions statute to relax the demands on electronic signatures. The Law of the Kyrgyz Republic about the Digital Signature, 2017 provides more flexibility in the use of what it calls "simple" electronic signatures.[174] Arrangements are also available for certificated digital signatures in appropriate cases as prescribed by law.[175] The law defines an electronic signature in very much the same way the MLEC (footnote 18) does, but the law provides for three kinds of electronic signature: simple, unqualified enhanced, and qualified enhanced.[176] The simple e-signature is "an electronic signature, the signature key of which coincides with the electronic signature itself (codes, passwords and other identifiers)."[177] An unqualified (enhanced) e-signature is one that meets conditions very like those that the MLEC presumes make an e-signature reliable. In addition, such a signature is created by cryptographic key. A qualified (enhanced) e-signature has the characteristics of the unqualified one, plus its signing key is indicated in a qualified certificate, which is one issued by an accredited certification center.[178]

Parties to a transaction may agree to use simple signatures to meet legal signing requirements and may presumably agree on the degree of reliability (including the type of technology) that they will accept for this purpose. Simple signatures may not be used to sign documents containing state secrets. A qualified e-signature is the equivalent of a handwritten signature unless the law prohibits using e-documents for the purpose.[179] The use of electronic documents and the classes of e-signatures for state bodies are governed by the Law of the Kyrgyz Republic about Electronic Control.[180]

Foreign signatures and certificates. The Kyrgyz Republic's statute reflects the MLES (footnote 20) in its rules on recognition of foreign signatures. There is no discrimination against an e-signature or e-document solely because the signature certificate "is issued in accordance with the law of a foreign state". An e-signature created under foreign law standards is recognized as the equivalent of a Kyrgyz signature of the same sort.[181] While the statute does not expressly focus on the similarity of the level of reliability of the foreign e-signature, that seems likely to be the focus of any inquiry.

In 2020, the government issued an order on the recognition of cross-border electronic signatures to implement a decision of the Eurasian Economic Union (EAEU).[182] It assigns duties to the State Customs Service and the State Committee on Information Technologies and Communications to ensure that electronic signatures by businesses conform with international standards and to see that e-documents submitted to other EAEU states are properly created. The role and function of state CSPs are harmonized with those of the EAEU as well.

---

[174] Government of the Kyrgyz Republic. 2017. *Law of the Kyrgyz Republic about the Digital Signature.* Bishkek. https://cis-legislation.com/document.fwx?rgn=99019.

[175] Automated translation of this statute (and presumably others) sometimes produces the phrase "electronic signature" and sometimes "digital signature" for the same Russian original. The Kyrgyz Republic statute consistently uses the word электронный, which properly is "electronic." The Russian for "digital" is цифровой. Both words are used in statutes with the phrase "electronic digital signature," common in CAREC laws but not in the Kyrgyz Republic. Since in careful usage and this report, a digital signature is a cryptographic subset of electronic signatures, one needs to pay attention to the original text at times—although CAREC usage does not give the plain phrase "digital signature" any cryptographic content.

[176] Footnote 174, Article 5(1).

[177] It seems likely that this definition would apply to a name typed at the bottom of an e-mail—an "other identifier".

[178] Footnote 174, Articles 1(3), and 5(2) through 5(4).

[179] Footnote 174, Articles 6(1) and 9(5).

[180] Government of the Kyrgyz Republic. 2017 (amended 2020). *Law of the Kyrgyz Republic about Electronic* Control. Bishkek. http://cis-legislation.com/document.fwx?rgn=99015.

[181] Footnote 174, Articles 7(1) and 7(2).

[182] Government of the Kyrgyz Republic. 2020. *Order No. 233 about authorized bodies of the Kyrgyz Republic on confirmation of electronic documents in case of cross-border information exchange of subjects of electronic interaction.* Bishkek. https://cis-legislation.com/document.fwx?rgn=124656.

Privacy. Privacy is protected principally through Law of the Kyrgyz Republic about Information of Personal Nature, 2008, which was amended in 2017 as the Law on Personal Data.[183] This is a modern and comprehensive statute with the usual features of such legislation.

Cross-border transfer of personal data. The law as amended allows for cross-border transfers of personal information if there is a treaty with the destination country that ensures an equivalent level of protection for the information. If such protection is lacking, the transfer may occur only with the consent of the data subject, or if it is needed for protection of that person's interest or confidentiality or if the information is in a public array of personal data.[184]

Cybercrime. Crimes involving computers are dealt with in articles 289–291 of the Criminal Code of the Kyrgyz Republic. The Code prohibits unauthorized access to computers; and erasing, modifying, or copying information as well as spreading of malwares. As in Kazakh legislation, whose provisions are very similar on all points, an offense by a group or an insider abusing his or her position is treated more severely. Penalties involve being denied access to computers. But the "same action [producing] imprudently grave consequences is punished with imprisonment [for] up to four years".[185]

A coordination center for ensuring cybersecurity to oversee government and public activities in this field was set up by government order in 2020 to share expertise domestically and internationally in fighting cybercrime, with particular reference to state bodies.[186]

Consumer protection. The Kyrgyz Republic has a detailed Law on the Protection of Consumer Rights that dates from 1997, though it has been updated frequently since then.[187] It provides standards of conduct for sellers and manufacturers, and provides private and public remedies for breaches of the standards. It prohibits a number of contractual provisions that prejudice consumers, including a ban on using electronic money. Its language is media neutral, so most of it can readily apply to online transactions. Electronic commerce is referred to only in remote sales, where "the Internet" is mentioned as one of several ways in which a consumer may learn about a product or service other than at the place of business of the merchant. In addition, standard prohibitions against fraud, forgery, and misrepresentation would apply to consumer transactions.[188]

Mongolia

Electronic transactions. Mongolia has very few specific rules for specific kinds of commercial documents.[189] An electronic document can (in principle) be used freely in cross-border trade under Mongolia's law. The Civil Code has been changed to make room for electronic transactions.[190] Mongolia has advanced its efforts toward electronic commerce. In December 2020, Mongolia acceded to the UN ECC (footnote 80).[191]

---

[183]   Government of the Kyrgyz Republic. 2008 (amended 2017). *Law of the Kyrgyz Republic about Information of Personal Nature.* Bishkek. http://cis-legislation.com/document.fwx?rgn=22274#A000000012.

[184]   Footnote 183, Articles 24 and 25.

[185]   Government of the Kyrgyz Republic. 1997 (as amended). *Criminal Code of the Kyrgyz Republic.* Bishkek. http://www.ilo.org/dyn/natlex/docs/ ELECTRONIC/67156/104401/F1696552027/KGZ67156%20Eng.pdf (Unofficial translation).

[186]   Government of the Kyrgyz Republic. 2020. *Order No. 266 about some questions in the field of ensuring cyber security.* Bishkek. https://cis-legislation. com/document.fwx?rgn=124892.

[187]   Government of the Kyrgyz Republic. 1997 (as amended to date). *Law on the Protection of Consumer Rights.* Bishkek. http://cbd.minjust.gov.kg/act/ view/ru-ru/590 (in Russian).

[188]   Footnote 187, Articles 24 and 27.

[189]   The study's analysis of Mongolia's legislation draws heavily from ESCAP. 2019. *Readiness Assessment for Cross-Border Paperless Trade: Mongolia.* Bangkok (footnote 54).

[190]   Mongolia enacted Article 42 of the Civil Code and added a provision to the indicia of a concluded transaction in Article 43.

[191]   It enters into effect for Mongolia on 1 July 2021.

The Law of Mongolia on Electronic Signature dates from 2011, with more recent amendments.[192] A contract that needs to be signed in writing must have some kind of electronic signature—but not necessarily a digital signature—if the contract is to be done electronically. An electronic signature is said to have the legal value of a handwritten signature, unless otherwise provided. State bodies must use digital signatures to sign electronically. There are no other specific rules in the Civil Code or other legislation about the form or content of an electronic document. Contracts that used to need to be in writing can be electronic.[193]

For digital signatures, it appears that the cryptographic key pair can be created by the signatory itself, but it is often issued by an agency known under Mongolia's law as a license holder. There are detailed regulations about how to issue a certificate and ensure it is accurate and up to date.[194]

Foreign signatures and certificates. A certificate issued "according to relevant foreign legislation" can be used in Mongolia. Nothing is said about standards for the content of the foreign legislation, or the criteria for being "relevant." License holders issuing certificates in Mongolia are to use internationally recognized technology and follow both national and international standards in their activity. This rule, properly followed, could help harmonize approaches and make foreign certificates easier to use in Mongolia, and vice versa. Further, the state administrative authority may "cooperate with foreign country and international organizations" to accommodate PKI activity of a foreign country into national PKI activity.[195]

Privacy. Mongolia has a privacy law dating from 1995, the Law About Personal Secrets.[196] It is a rudimentary statute that names a few kinds of personal "secrets" and prohibits the disclosure of "information, documents and tangible things that may be detrimental to the person's legitimate interests, dignity and reputation."[197] There is nothing in the statute about the consent of the data subject, or about informing the person about the purpose of the collection. No rights of access or correction are given to individuals whose secrets are disclosed or collected. The unlawful acquiring and disclosing personal secrets without consent is subject to criminal sanction.[198]

Cybercrime. The Criminal Code of Mongolia has several provisions about crimes relating to security of computer data or electronic information.[199] Among the prohibited acts under the code are illegal access of data using "electronic device and information network" and deletion, modification or duplication of information, and limiting access to or illegal transfer of computer data that cause damage to legal interests of others. The penalty is higher for these acts if committed by "organized criminal groups" or "committed against state secret or crucial information and network."[200] In addition, developing and selling special program and device to facilitate such illegal access; and creation, use, and spread of malware are also punishable acts.[201]

Consumer protection. Mongolia's Law on Consumer Protection protects consumers in the "sale, purchase, performance of works and provision of services of goods and products."[202] The law underlines requirements for

---

[192] Government of Mongolia. 2011. *Law of Mongolia About Electronic Signatures* (as amended to 2018). Ulaanbaatar. https://www.legalinfo.mn/law/details/574?lawid=574. (in Mongolian). See also Government of Mongolia, Communications Regulatory Commission. 2011. *Law of Mongolia on Electronic Signature.* http://www.crc.gov.mn/en/k/2lq/1q.

[193] Footnote 192, Articles 5.1 and 6.3.

[194] Government of Mongolia, Communications Regulatory Commission. 2014. *Procedures for Public Key Infrastructure for Mongolia's Digital Signature,* Regulation 2014-45. Ulaanbaatar. http://www.crc.gov.mn/k/BG (in Mongolian).

[195] Footnote 192, Articles 17, 29.2.9 through 10 and 33.1.3.

[196] Government of Mongolia, 1995. *Law about Personal Secrets.* Ulaanbaatar. https://www.legalinfo.mn/law/details/537 (in Mongolian).

[197] Footnote 196.

[198] An Overview of Mongolia's Data Protection is discussed in this article: C. Melville and E. Odkhuu. 2020. *Mongolia: Data Protection Overview Guidance Note.* https://www.dataguidance.com/notes/mongolia-data-protection-overview.

[199] Government of Mongolia. 2013. *Criminal Code of Mongolia (as amended in 2018).* Ulaanbaatar. https://www.legalinfo.mn/law/details/15901?lawid=15901.

[200] Footnote 199, Article 26.1.

[201] Footnote 199, Articles 26.2 and 26.3.

[202] Government of Mongolia, 2003. *Law on Consumer Protection (as amended in 2015).* Ulaanbaatar. https://www.legalinfo.mn/law/details/551 (in Mongolian).

quality and safety, need for accurate information, and rights to compensation of damages caused by fault of producers, sellers, and contractors. The law further provides that "if an international treaty to which Mongolia is a party provides otherwise than this law, the provisions of the international treaty shall prevail."[203] Although not explicitly stated, the law may be applicable to online sales.

Pakistan

As a national priority, Pakistan adopted an e-commerce policy in 2019 to create an enabling environment for holistic growth of e-commerce across all sectors of the country, including plans for national single window and cross-border e-commerce.[204]

Electronic transactions. Pakistan adopted an Electronic Transactions Ordinance in 2002; there is no available information of any update during this study.[205] The ordinance is quite different from the laws of other CAREC members. It adopts large parts of the MLEC (footnote 18).[206] The ordinance indicates that the requirement for signatures "shall be deemed satisfied" where electronic signatures or advanced electronic signatures are applied".[207] The ordinance does not require either evidence of intention or any degree of reliability. However, reliability is supported by the use of an "advanced electronic signature." With such a signature, it is presumed that the signed document is authentic and has integrity; or that the signature is that of the person to whom it correlates, it was affixed for the purpose of signing or approving the document, and the e-document has not been altered since it was signed.[208]

An advanced e-signature can be made in two ways. The first is to create it in the circumstances which the MLES says makes for a reliable signature (footnote 20, Article 6[3]). The second is to have it created by an accredited CSP considered by a government supervisory agency—the Electronic Certification Accreditation Council (ECAC)—to be capable of establishing authenticity and integrity. Not all CSPs need to be accredited.[209] Detailed regulations govern the accreditation process.[210] The ordinance describes in detail the composition of the ECAC and its functions.[211] Public bodies—known as "appropriate authority" in the ordinance—may accept or reject electronic documents and payments. If they decide to accept them, the authorities may specify the technology and the process to ensure the integrity of the information received.[212] They are not in a position to negotiate the format, so the ordinance gives them the power to impose it.

Foreign signatures and certificates. The regulator of the accreditation system, the ECAC, is allowed to recognize or accredit foreign CSPs.[213] The ordinance does not indicate the grounds on which such arrangements might be made or whether they should be reciprocal. The ECAC's Accreditation Regulations say that a CSP

203 Footnote 202, Article 2.2.
204 Government of Pakistan, Commerce Division. 2019. *E-Commerce Policy of Pakistan.* Islamabad. http://www.commerce.gov.pk/wp-content/uploads/2019/11/e-Commerce_Policy_of_Pakistan_Print.pdf.
205 Government of Pakistan. 2002. *Electronic Transactions Ordinance.* Islamabad. https://www.ecac.org.pk/assets/front/files/eto2002.pdf.
206 Pakistan is the only CAREC country other than the PRC to be listed by the UN Commission on International Trade Law (UNCITRAL) as having implemented the MLEC. UNCITRAL. UNCITRAL Model Law on Electronic Commerce (1996) - Status. https://uncitral.un.org/en/texts/ecommerce/modellaw/electronic_commerce/status (accessed 8 August 2020).
207 Footnote 205, Section 7.
208 Footnote 205, Section 9. It is not clear why the two sets of presumptions are joined by "or". One would have thought that both presumptions might apply to any e-document so signed, and both could be important.
209 Footnote 205, Section 2(a) and 17.
210 Government of Pakistan, Ministry of Information Technology and Telecom, ECAC. 2008. *The Certification Service Providers' Accreditation Regulations, 2008.* Islamabad. https://www.ecac.org.pk/assets/front/files/The%20Certification%20Service%20Providers'%20Accreditation%20Regulations,%202008%20updated.pdf.
211 Footnote 205, Sections 18 through 25.
212 Footnote 205, Section 13.
213 Footnote 205, Section 21(2)(f).

formed in another country can get permission under corporate law to carry on business in Pakistan, and then apply for accreditation.[214]

Privacy. Pakistan does not have a privacy statute of general application. The ordinance allows the ECAC to make regulations about privacy and the protection of personal data of subscribers to signature certificates from CSPs.[215] The Prevention of Electronic Crimes Act of 2016 prohibits the unauthorized obtaining, sale, possession, transmission, or use of a person's "identity information."[216] A person who has been the victim of such activities may apply to the Pakistan Telecommunication Authority to have the information secured, blocked, or prevented from being further transmitted. The National Database and Registration Authority, which maintains records for all citizens of Pakistan and runs the national identity card program, has strict rules about keeping its information confidential.[217]

Cross-border transfer of personal data. Cross-border sharing of personal data is more likely to be focused on the same security priorities than on protecting individuals from undue commercial exploitation.

Cybercrime. The ordinance prohibits entering computer systems to see or take the information in them—a provision headed "violation of privacy of information," although it is not in the nature of personal data protection. It also bans and penalizes causing damage to information systems.[218]

The principal source of cybercrime law is the Prevention of Electronic Crimes Act of 2016.[219] This statute prohibits most or all of the activities that the Budapest Convention of 2001 (footnote 33) requires member states to ban: unauthorized access to information systems, unauthorized copying of data, interference with an information system (particularly with regard to critical infrastructure systems), forgery, fraud, supplying of malware devices, spamming, spoofing, and several others. It focuses as well on offenses relating to terrorism, including "cyber-terrorism"—that is, using e-communications for spreading fear or inciting hate, "glorification" of terrorism, hate speech, and recruiting for terrorism. The act contains an array of procedural rights and techniques used to fight cybercrime. It is by far the most extensive legislation on this topic among CAREC members. It allows for anticipatory action and censorship, including removing content from information systems by the decision of the Pakistan Telecommunication Authority. The act contains a substantial set of provisions about cooperating with foreign countries (both for collecting information and for sharing it) for the purpose of investigation or prosecution of electronic crimes.[220] Pakistan may also refuse to accede to a foreign government's request for a number of reasons, including that Pakistan's interests would be prejudiced and that the request was made for an improper purpose.

Consumer protection. Pakistan has no national consumer protection statute. Each of its provinces, including the capital region, has a statute on the topic, but most of them were enacted in the 1990s or earlier and do not apply directly to electronic commerce. The legislation focuses mainly on the safety of consumer products being sold in the provinces.[221]

---

[214]   Footnote 210, Section 3(4).

[215]   Footnote 205, Section 43(2)(e).

[216]   Government of Pakistan. 2016. An Act to make provisions for prevention of electronic crimes. Islamabad. http://www.nr3c.gov.pk/peca16.pdf.

[217]   Government of Pakistan. 2000. The National Database and Registration Authority Ordinance, 2000. Islamabad. http://nasirlawsite.com/laws/nadra.htm.

[218]   Footnote 205, Sections 36 and 37.

[219]   Footnote 216.

[220]   Footnote 216, Sections 37 and 42.

[221]   A useful overview of consumer protection in Pakistan was given to an UNCTAD workshop in 2016. Government of Pakistan, Competition Commission of Pakistan. 2016. Capacity Building in Consumer Protection: Trends and Challenges. Report prepared for the UNCTAD Intergovernmental Group of Experts on Consumer Protection Law and Policy, First Session. Geneva. 17–18 October. https://unctad.org/meetings/en/Contribution/ciclp2016c03_ccPakistan_en.pdf.

The province of Sindh is the exception, with a consumer protection statute enacted in 2015.[222] It deals with safety issues, but also with misrepresentation and warranties. It was drafted in media-neutral language so could apply to e-commerce transactions. However, the only express reference to such transactions is in the definition of "advertising," which includes internet communications, short message service, and other electronic media. Typical online consumer protection measures found elsewhere, like the right to receive a contract within a short time of the transaction or rescission rights, are not mentioned.

Tajikistan

The Concept of the Digital Economy in the Republic of Tajikistan has been developed, which provides for the improvement of the environment for the development of electronic commerce in the country. In 2020, Tajikistan also launched its single window system for registration of an export, import, and transit procedure.

Electronic transactions. Tajikistan has two principal statutes that affect electronic transactions, one on electronic documents and another on electronic digital signatures. The Law of the Republic of Tajikistan about Electronic Documents (2002, amended in 2014) allows an electronic document to be the functional equivalent of a written document.[223] The electronic document must "contain the details allowing to identify it", but it does not need an electronic digital signature or a certificate of any kind to serve that purpose.[224] The law says that the "special part" of an e-document "consists of one or several electronic digital signatures or other means which are identifying the originator, and not contradicting the legislation of the Republic of Tajikistan." The "other means" need not be such a signature, so any reasonable evidence of origin would suffice.[225] Participants in e-document systems may operate abroad and make agreements with foreign entities and use international communications networks according to Tajikistan law and its treaties.[226]

The Law of the Republic of Tajikistan about the Electronic Digital Signature (2007, amended in 2011) governs how those signatures work.[227] It says at the outset that it does not apply to any other alternatives to a handwritten signature.[228] This disclaimer suggests that transacting parties, especially private parties, may be free to devise other alternatives that suit their purposes—always subject to proof of attribution and intention. The law defines an "enterprise (or corporate) information system" as a small, centrally controlled group constituted by one person or by agreement of the group. In comparison to Azerbaijan and Georgia, where a similar provision exists, such a group was allowed to use its own authentication methods. The law states that the use of uncertificated electronic digital signatures with electronic documents for such an information system is not allowed.[229] However, so long as the corporate information system is not relying on a certification center for its own electronic digital certificates, this suggests that a narrow opening to greater flexibility at least may allow some productive experimentation at a low risk of loss.[230]

---

[222] Provincial Assembly of Sindh. 2015. *The Sindh Consumer Protection Act, 2014*. Karachi. http://www.pas.gov.pk/index.php/acts/details/en/31/284. The official title includes "2014," though the final enactment occurred in 2015.
[223] Government of Tajikistan. 2002 (amended 2014). *Law of the Republic of Tajikistan about Electronic Documents*. Dushanbe. http://cis-legislation.com/document.fwx?rgn=2183. Article 11.
[224] Footnote 223, Article 6.
[225] Footnote 223, Article 8.
[226] Footnote 223, Article 25.
[227] Government of Tajikistan. 2007 (amended 2011). *Law of the Republic of Tajikistan about the Electronic Digital Signature*. Dushanbe. http://cis-legislation.com/document.fwx?rgn=18412.
[228] Footnote 227, Article 1.
[229] Footnote 227, Article 6.
[230] Footnote 227, Article 22.

The Law of the Republic of Tajikistan about the Electronic Digital Signature describes the organization and duties of certification centers.[231] Some of the demands are similar to the trustworthiness rules of the MLES (footnote 20).[232] Public authorities of Tajikistan use certified electronic digital signatures. The statute describes how they allocate the responsibility among the individuals in an office.[233] At present, businesses and consumers do use electronic communications to make contracts and to make payments.

Foreign certificates. The Law of the Republic of Tajikistan about the Electronic Digital Signature also provides for the recognition of a foreign signature key certificate "in accordance with the current legislation of the Republic of Tajikistan and international treaties recognized by Tajikistan."[234]

Privacy. Tajikistan adopted the Law about Personal Data Protection in 2018.[235] Its content are similar to other CAREC laws on the topic. Biometric information is particularly sensitive and cannot be collected without the written consent of the subject, except those in the list of instances in which biometric data may be collected and shared.[236] The state oversees the system and can enforce people's obligations to protect privacy.[237]

Cross-border transfer of personal data. Personal data from Tajikistan can be shared outside the country to places that have adequate protection for privacy, except that Tajikistan can restrict such sharing for a number of broadly stated reasons.[238]

Cybercrime. Tajikistan has a longer list of computer-related prohibitions than any other of its CAREC neighbors. The Criminal Code of the Republic of Tajikistan has what seem to be the usual provisions on gaining unauthorized access to computers, harming the content of computers, distributing malware, and abusing authorized access, though spelled out in more detail than is done elsewhere.[239] The criminal code also prohibits illegal appropriation through copying or compulsion to transmit information through blackmail by threatening to divulge "discreditable data" about somebody, or through violence.[240] Creating hacking equipment and programs are separately prohibited from distributing malware.[241]

Consumer protection. Although standard prohibitions against fraud, forgery, and misrepresentation would apply to consumer transactions, there appear to be no laws specifically directed at protecting online or offline consumers.

---

[231] Footnote 227, Articles 9 through 13.
[232] Footnote 227, Articles 14 through 20.
[233] Footnote 227, Article 21.
[234] Footnote 227, Article 23.
[235] Government of Tajikistan. 2018. Law of the Republic of Tajikistan about Personal Data Protection. Dushanbe. http://cis-legislation.com/document.fwx?rgn=108952.
[236] Footnote 235, Article 17.
[237] Footnote 235, Articles 5 through 7.
[238] Footnote 235, Article 18.
[239] Government of Tajikistan.1998 (amended 2020), *Criminal Code of Tajikistan*. Dushanbe. https://cis-legislation.com/document.fwx?rgn=2324.
[240] Footnote 239, Article 301.
[241] Footnote 239, Article 302.

Turkmenistan

Electronic transactions. Electronic signatures and documents are governed by the 2020 Law of Turkmenistan about the Electronic Document, Electronic Document Management and Digital Services.[242] It is a comprehensive statute that describes a number of digital activities in detail. Some parts of the 2020 statute are similar to the MLEC (footnote 18), such as the provisions on the sending and receipt of documents, electronic evidence, and storage.

The main provisions on electronic documents require that such documents be authenticated with an electronic digital signature. This is a signature based on public key cryptography, with a private key to encrypt and sign the document and a public key by which it can be read and at the same time authenticated. There are detailed rules about how certificates are created and used to link the public key with the owner of the signature key. The government can accredit a number of CSPs, called "centers of registration," whose duties are spelled out in the statute.[243]

However, it is possible for transacting parties to choose more flexible and less technically demanding electronic communications. The main rules do not apply to documents authenticated by scanned handwritten signatures or other methods that do not use electronic digital signatures.[244] In addition, electronic digital signatures appear to be permitted under private rules in "corporate (or enterprise) information systems," defined as systems with "certain participants" this appears to be mean closed systems, in which all participants are known. Such systems may spell out their own rules, but they are still electronic digital signatures that operate as contemplated by the law.[245]

The 2020 law (footnote 242) also describes the offer of "digital services," including digital trading. Electronic payments are subject to the rules of the Central Bank of Turkmenistan. The whole system is overseen by the Cabinet of Ministers, with day-to-day operations the responsibility of the "authorized state body" not otherwise named in the statute.[246]

Foreign signatures and certificates. Electronic documents created under the rules of a foreign state or under international standards will be recognized in Turkmenistan either if based on treaties signed by Turkmenistan or if governed by private agreements that conform to Turkmenistan law. An electronic digital signature with a foreign certificate is recognized if so provided by Turkmenistan's international treaties.[247]

Privacy. Many provisions of the 2020 law (footnote 242) require protection of personal data in different situations. These provisions often refer to this protection "according to the legislation of Turkmenistan", "according to the legislation and international treaties", or "according to the legislation of Turkmenistan on personal data and their protection".[248] Traders may ask only for personal information needed for the transaction on digital trading. There are additional provisions on private protection as well as legal remedies for violations of privacy.[249]

---

[242] Government of Turkmenistan. 2020. Law of Turkmenistan about the Electronic Document, Electronic Document Management and Digital Services. Ashgabat. https://cis-legislation.com/document.fwx?rgn=123179. The text of the law frequently leaves detailed rules or exceptions to "the legislation of Turkmenistan," either on particular topics like information security support (Article 26[2]) or cryptographic protective equipment (Article 27[3]), or just in general (e.g., articles 27[2], 30, 34[3]).
[243] Footnote 242, Articles 39 through 48.
[244] Footnote 242, Articles 3(3) and 3(4). One difficulty in using anything but an electronic digital signature on a document in electronic form is that Article 1 defines such a document as being authenticated by an electronic digital signature. In the light of that definition, it is hard to understand the apparent permission to use other authentication methods. This problem demonstrates that substantive rules of law (e.g., how to authenticate an e-document) should not be put in a definition.
[245] Footnote 242, Articles 1(27), and 36(1) through 36(3).
[246] Footnote 242, Articles 49, 52, 54, and 55.
[247] Footnote 242, Article 17.
[248] Footnote 242, Articles 11(2), 34(4), and 46(1).
[249] Footnote 242, Articles 53(11)(3) and 56(3).

Cybercrime. Turkmenistan has two provisions in its criminal code that resemble those in other CAREC countries: Article 334 on unauthorized access to computers and doing harm while there, and Article 335 on distributing malware. Like the others, they impose more severe penalties on groups or other specially motivated offenders. Turkmenistan also has a provision (Article 333) that protects computer-related technology as a kind of intellectual property provision.[250]

Consumer protection. Standard prohibitions against fraud, forgery, and misrepresentation would apply to consumer transactions. "Sellers must provide all information about the goods (works, services) they offer in a form that allows their addressee, who does not have special knowledge, unambiguously [to] identify the information received as related to electronic commerce and form a reliable idea of the legal status of the person engaged in electronic commerce, his goods (works, services), their prices and the terms of their purchase."[251]

Uzbekistan

Uzbekistan has been moving on several fronts to promote electronic commerce. In 2019, the United Nations (UN) Economic and Social Commission for Asia and the Pacific (ESCAP) published a report on its legal, technological, and business readiness for cross-border paperless trade, which is referred to in the analysis of Uzbekistan's legislations.[252]

Electronic transactions. Uzbekistan has several statutes that affect electronic transactions: the Law about Electronic Signatures,[253] the Law about Electronic Commerce,[254] and the Law about Electronic Document Management.[255] Legal effect is also given to presidential decrees and proclamations, and resolutions of the Cabinet of Ministers. It would be useful to keep track of these developments in legal infrastructure and have them consolidated.

The Law about Electronic Commerce (footnote 254) is very supportive of electronic commerce and seems to offer greater flexibility in how one creates documents and signatures. On the other hand, the Cabinet of Ministers Resolution No. 185 of 2016 set out quite detailed requirements for electronic contract, though often in technology-neutral language.[256] Different legal instruments of different levels of authority may contain contradictory rules and should be avoided to the extent possible.

Foreign certificates. The Law about Electronic Digital Signatures says that "the use of certificates of keys of electronic digital signatures of foreign states is performed according to the procedure established by the legislation."[257]

250 Government of Turkmenistan, *Criminal Code of Turkmenistan.* 1997 (amended 2020) Ashgabat. I http://cis-legislation.com/document-original.fwx?rgn=2420.
251 Footnote 242, Article 53(5).
252 Footnote 54.
253 Government of Uzbekistan. 2003 (amended 2018). *Law about Electronic Digital Signatures.* Tashkent. http://cis-legislation.com/document.fwx?rgn=11889.
254 Government of Uzbekistan. 2004 (amended 2017). *Law about Electronic Commerce.* Tashkent. http://cis-legislation.com/document.fwx?rgn=6591.
255 Government of Uzbekistan. 2004. *Law about Electronic Document Management.* http://cis-legislation.com/document.fwx?rgn=6592.
256 Government of Uzbekistan. 2016 (amended 2018). *Resolution No. 185 of the Cabinet of Ministers of the Republic of Uzbekistan about measures for further enhancement of procedure of transactions in electronic commerce.* Tashkent. http://cis-legislation.com/document.fwx?rgn=86244.
257 Footnote 253, Article 19. It is not clear what legislation is being referred to.

Privacy. Uzbekistan enacted a privacy statute, the Law about Personal Data, in 2019.[258] Its provisions are in the modern mainstream of such legislation. A novel and interesting provision protects people from having decisions made based on their personal data being subjected to "automated personal data processing", which likely means decisions made based on artificial intelligence or machine learning.[259]

As in several other CAREC countries, there is a state register of databases of personal data. Enforcement is in the hands of the State Personalization Center. While the state guarantees the protection of personal data, this does not relieve the owner or operator of data systems of their responsibilities to comply with the statute. It appears that the statute applies to the state's own collection of personal information. The Cabinet of Ministers is to bring governmental practices in line with the law.[260]

Cross-border transfer of personal data. Personal data may be transferred out of Uzbekistan if the country of destination provides equivalent protection for them. Otherwise, data may be transferred with the consent of the subject, or for public order or public health purposes, or based on applicable treaties (if any). The statute also lists several reasons for which export of data is prohibited.[261]

Cybercrime. Uzbekistan prohibits crimes related to information technology in the Criminal Code of the Republic of Uzbekistan.[262] It is similar to most CAREC legislation which lists prohibited acts or violation on information access, such as "illegal or unauthorized access to computer information," creation, use and spread of malware, development of "software or hardware" for illegal access of "protected computer system or telecommunications network" for "purposes of marketing", "modification of computer information" that cause major damage or harm to citizens or public interests, and "computer sabotage". In addition, the Law about Electronic Commerce provides that an information intermediary shall "provide with measures of protection electronic documents, electronic messages and personal data from unauthorized access."[263]

Consumer protection. Uzbekistan enacted the Law about Consumer Protection in 1996 and updated it in 2019.[264] It sets out the rules for good conduct—full and timely disclosure of contract terms, the requirement that goods be safe and fit for their purpose, and the requirement that services be performed according to the contract for them—and provides for remedies both at the hands of state agencies and in court. In 2019, a presidential decree established the Agency for the Protection of Consumer Rights to coordinate all state bodies in the field of consumer protection.[265]

The consumer protection statute does not mention electronic transactions at all, but its provisions are in media-neutral language that can readily be applied to such transactions. Moreover, the Law about Electronic Commerce requires the "participant in electronic commerce" (the seller), to "observe requirements of the legislation on ... competition and about consumer protection in case of sales of goods (works, services) in electronic commerce".[266] In short, the Law about Electronic Commerce ensures that the rules of the consumer protection legislation apply online as well.

---

[258]   Government of Uzbekistan. 2019. *Law about Personal Data*. Tashkent. http://cis-legislation.com/document.fwx?rgn=116961.

[259]   Footnote 258, Article 24. Some of the concerns involved in such an analysis are described in J. Gregory. 2017. *Proprietary Algorithms for Public Purposes*. Slaw. 24 July. http://www.slaw.ca/2017/07/24/proprietary-algorithms-for-public-purposes/.

[260]   Footnote 258, Articles 20, 27, and 35.

[261]   Footnote 258, Article 15.

[262]   Government of the Republic of Uzbekistan. 1994 (amended, 2020). *Criminal Code of the Republic of Uzbekistan Tashkent*. https://lex.uz/docs/111457. Article 278, (1) through (7). This should be read with the Government of the Republic of Uzbekistan. 2004. *Law about Informatization 2004*. (amended 2021). Tashkent. https://lex.uz/docs/82956.

[263]   Footnote 254, Article 13.

[264]   Government of Uzbekistan. 1996 (amended 2019). *Law about Consumer Protection*. Tashkent. https://cis-legislation.com/document.fwx?rgn=909.

[265]   Government of Uzbekistan. 2019. *Decree No. 5817 of the President of the Republic of Uzbekistan: On measures to radically improve the legal and institutional system of consumer protection*. Tashkent. 11 September.

[266]   Footnote 254, Article 11.

6 Additional Considerations

Governments wishing to promote e-commerce need to be aware of the context in which it will operate. The interim conclusions of the United Nations Conference on Trade and Development (UNCTAD) from its rapid e-readiness studies of least-developed countries may be of interest and inspire countries further along the development path in this respect. Besides putting the missing legislative links into place, UNCTAD recommends that countries should:

(i)   build capacities of lawmakers and judiciary (and civil servants);

(ii)   strengthen business and civil society engagement;

(iii) promote quality labels and certification trust-mark schemes (as extralegal trust supports);

(iv)   increase awareness of e-commerce regulations and consumer protection measures;

(v)   develop policies on data server localization, data protection, data transfer across borders, and taxation; and

(vi)   coordinate all of the above.[267]

As the Asian Development Bank (ADB) and UN Economic and Social Commission for Asia and the Pacific (ESCAP) argue, the barriers to e-commerce in developing countries can be—besides legal—economic, institutional, or social.[268] They can involve the levels of awareness, knowledge, skills, and confidence of both the internet buyer and seller. Among the types of barriers potential e-traders may encounter are:

(i)   customs duties, procedures, and administration;

(ii)   limited and lack of harmonization in consumer and sales law and information;

(iii) different and a lack of tailored payment and tax treatment of e-commerce;

(iv)   inadequate or varied intellectual property rights and protection;

(v)   obstacles to cross-border information and data transfer;

(vi)   restrictive state controls; and

(vii) various issues of fraud, insurance, product certification, regulation of standards, and rules of origin.

Transparency. Domestic and cross-border e-commerce depends on trust and thus requires transparency in the interactions of all the participants. Paperless trade offers economic and legal benefits. It reduces the number of person-to-person dealings, creates an auditable record from one end of the transaction to the other, and promotes regulatory compliance.[269] However, going paperless is a slow process that is sometimes resisted, left incomplete, and subjected to claims that it raises the risks of fraud.

---

[267]   UNCTAD. 2019. Rapid eTrade Readiness Assessment of Least Developed Countries: Policy Impact and Way Forward. https://unctad.org/en/PublicationsLibrary/dtlstict2019d7_en.pdf.

[268]   Footnote 5.

[269]   See for example the United Nations Economic and Social Commission for Asia and the Pacific's Framework Agreement on Facilitation of Cross-Border Paperless Trade in Asia and the Pacific. The phrase "regulatory compliance" appears six times in the text of the agreement and in the explanatory note, including in the third recital: "Recognizing that paperless trade makes international trade more efficient and transparent while improving regulatory compliance, particularly if trade-related data and documents in electronic form are exchanged across borders…" (footnote 86, p. 1).

7 Recommendations

Although most of the e-commerce statutes of the Central Asia Regional Economic Cooperation (CAREC) countries adhere to common principles, some differ in ways that are not explained by either principle or local conditions. This forces parties to navigate 11 distinct legal regimes if they want to engage in e-commerce and to deal with the higher costs and potential for confusion that result. The harmonization of CAREC country legislations on e-commerce would provide the benefits of efficiency and predictability. A common statutory approach would also make consultation on and drafting national legislation easier.

The development by the CAREC members of a suite of common e-commerce laws could serve as a framework to help build consumer and commercial trust in electronic transactions. Such a framework would serve as a strong statement by governments to the region's businesses and consumers that it is safe to engage in e-commerce, and that governments will not be a barrier. This is not to say that one size fits all with respect to legislation across CAREC members. Their economies and societies often differ substantially, as does their capacity to achieve law reform. But having a clear goal of integration can make developing the necessary laws easier. Tables 9 and 10 list a summary of recommended actions for domestic law reform and accession to or adoption of international instruments.

Table 9: Recommendations for Domestic Law Reform

Reform Needed	Countries	Remarks
Adopt the UN Convention on the Use of Electronic Communications in International Contracts (generally shortened to ECC)	All	The Parliament of Mongolia ratified the ECC in 2020
Maximize and harmonize ability to use simple e-signatures among CAREC countries	All	Some CAREC national laws have flexibility
Harmonize the certification process for digital signatures across the CAREC countries	All	Harmonization might be done by all copying the rules of the state whose system works best, or by adapting existing rules into a single version that will work for everybody State supervision is needed but it is not necessary to establish a state monopoly to achieve this.
Harmonize cybercrime legislation with international standards	All	CAREC laws' provisions are largely consistent; they should consider their capacity to enforce and further cooperation with other member states
Enact modern privacy legislation	Afghanistan, Mongolia, Pakistan	Consider state capacity to enforce any privacy rules that are enacted.

continued on next page

Reform Needed	Countries	Remarks
Enact modern consumer protection legislation	Pakistan, Tajikistan	Harmonize legislation based on UN guidelines for online consumer protection[a] All members to consider state capacity to enforce any consumer protection measures enacted. Join the International Consumer Protection and Enforcement Network

CAREC = Central Asia Regional Economic Cooperation, ECC = Electronic Communications Convention, UN = United Nations.

[a] UNCTAD. 2016. United Nations Guidelines for Consumer Protection. Geneva. https://unctad.org/en/PublicationsLibrary/ditccplpmisc2016d1_en.pdf. The guidelines are available in all official UN languages, notably Chinese and Russian. See also OECD.2016., Consumer Protection in E-commerce: OECD Recommendation, OECD Publishing, Paris. http://dx.doi.org/10.1787/9789264255258-en.

Source: Authors' compilation.

Table 10: Recommendations for Accession to or Adoption of International Instruments

Instrument	Type/ Scope	CAREC Membership and Recommended Actions
UN Convention on the Use of Electronic Communications in International Contracts (generally shortened to ECC)	Global	Azerbaijan and Mongolia are parties. The PRC is a signatory but has yet to ratify. The rest of the CAREC countries should join.
UN Framework Agreement on Facilitation of Cross-Border Paperless Trade in Asia and the Pacific	Regional	Azerbaijan acceded in March 2018 and the PRC ratified the agreement in November 2020. The agreement entered into force in February 2021. The rest of the CAREC countries are encouraged to join.
UN Convention on the International Sale of Goods	Global	Current: Azerbaijan, PRC, Georgia, Kyrgyz Republic, Mongolia, and Uzbekistan The rest of the CAREC countries should join.
WTO Trade Facilitation Agreement	Global	Current: Afghanistan, PRC, Georgia, Kazakhstan, Kyrgyz Republic, Mongolia, Pakistan, and Tajikistan The remaining three CAREC countries (Azerbaijan, Turkmenistan, and Uzbekistan) are at various stages of accession to the WTO.
WCO Revised Kyoto Customs Convention	Global	Current: Azerbaijan, PRC, Georgia, Kazakhstan, Mongolia, Pakistan, Tajikistan, Turkmenistan and Uzbekistan
Council of Europe Convention on Cybercrime (Budapest Convention of 2001)	Global	Current: Azerbaijan, Georgia
Customs Convention on the International Transport of Goods under Cover of TIR Carnets (TIR Convention) with Annex 11 on digital documents (in force May 2021)	Global	Current: All CAREC countries

CAREC = Central Asia Regional Economic Cooperation, ECC = Electronic Communications Convention, ESCAP = Economic and Social Commission for Asia and the Pacific, PRC = People's Republic of China, TIR = Transports Internationaux Routiers (International Road Transport), UN = United Nations, WCO = World Customs Organization, WTO = World Trade Organization.

Source: Authors' compilation.

Electronic Transactions

Domestic Application

All electronic transactions statutes should tell the same story: that it is acceptable in law to communicate electronically and to use e-documents and e-signatures to buy and sell goods and services. At present, those reading the legislation of some CAREC countries on e-commerce can get lost in the technical convolutions and inconsistencies. It also makes sense for countries to consider treating electronic documents and electronic signatures as a whole in legislation rather than having separate statutes for each as if they were unrelated topics. Some states—the People's Republic of China (PRC) and Uzbekistan, for example—have statutes that deal with e-commerce separately from the questions of authentication of documents and signatures in the usual legislation.

E-commerce statutes are valuable to the extent that they deal with matters that are distinct from and additional to those already addressed by the laws on offline commerce. If they simply repeat the law from elsewhere, they are less useful and may confuse readers.[270] Ideally, the legal concepts relevant to e-commerce should be the same as those relevant to any other commerce. The legislation should offer technology-neutral standards for those who are comfortable with them.[271] The principle of consent is essential—i.e., the principle that parties to voluntary transactions should be able to decide whether or not to undertake them electronically. If they believe that any element of the communications is insecure—the signature is not reliable, the text of the contract is not certain—then they can refuse to consent, or insist that the security be improved. In short, the parties can decide how secure they need to feel in order to rely on e-communications.[272]

The legislation can help parties know how to judge the reliability of electronic documents they are invited to use. This can be done by using some guidelines for presumptive reliability, such as the signature standards of Article 6(3) of the Model Law on Electronic Signatures (MLES). It may also be done—perhaps as a supplement to the technology-neutral standard—by providing a system of secure documentation: documents and signatures that can be certified as reliable by someone who meets state standards for performing such work. Those state standards can be prescribed by law—as the MLES does for certification service providers (CSPs) and other parties to secure communications—or can be overseen by state authorities.[273]

Essentially, a hybrid legislation, with "simple" e-documents and e-signatures and "secure" (or "enhanced" or "advanced") versions of them, is recommended. Most of the time, parties using the documents should be allowed to decide how much protection they require and what technology will provide it. That may involve highly secure methods but normally will not. However, the state may want to direct who uses what technology, such as in the following situation:

(i)   When members of the public and state bodies communicate electronically, both sides need to be confident that they are actually dealing with the party they think they are.[274]

---

[270]   Uzbekistan also has a law on electronic government. It tends to set out the security standards for communications between public bodies and residents, the use of single identifiers across ministries, and the like. Government of Uzbekistan. 2015. Law of the Republic of Uzbekistan about the Electronic Government. Tashkent. http://cis-legislation.com/document.fwx?rgn=81271.

[271]   The most efficient way to incorporate the United Nations Commission on International Trade Law (UNCITRAL) standards into domestic law may be to accede to the United Nations (UN) Electronic Communications Convention (ECC) and have it applied to domestic communications.

[272]   Communications with government may not give parties the option to decide on the medium of communications, since most communications with government are often compelled by law and not voluntary.

[273]   The MLES contemplates such an official status in Article 7.

[274]   While it is not strictly speaking a matter of e-commerce, it is very important that all parts of the state—ministries, agencies, and authorities—be legally capable of using e-communications with one another and the outside world. Such an ability should be made a matter of clear law that includes whatever provisions are appropriate to ensuring confidence in the reliability of the communications.

(ii)   Some members of the public will not be in a position to judge how reliable e-communications are. As a matter of consumer protection, the state may be justified in requiring that communications with these people be done either on paper or through a trusted third party. Such a decision should be open to periodic review, as more secure new technologies may emerge that lower the risks.

(iii)   As an alternative to step (ii), the state could require the use of secure communications for transactions above a certain value that acts as a marker for the cases that need protection.

(iv)   Businesspeople may also have different degrees of risk tolerance (and of risk appreciation). A statutory system of certificated signatures and providers (whether provided by the state or regulated by the state) should be open to anyone who wants to use it (possibly on paying a fee for the service).

The use of a secure system could be encouraged by making it a safe harbor technology. This means that if the system is used, the attribution of the signature or document will be presumed to be as it purports to be, or as it is asserted to be in the certificate. The technology-neutral equivalent is the presumption that someone signing in a way described in MLES Article 6(3) has signed validly. Pakistan law has a presumption in such a case that the signature is authentic, and that the document has integrity.[275] The Kyrgyz Republic provides for flexibility in simple electronic signatures (footnote 138). Within CAREC, one should study the relevant statutes of Azerbaijan and the PRC, both parties to the United Nations (UN) Electronic Communications Convention (ECC).

International Application

All CAREC member states that have not yet done so should accede to the ECC established by the United Nations Commission on International Trade Law (UNCITRAL) and apply it both internationally and domestically (footnote 80). Accession to the ECC opens up other conventions to which the member state is a party and so allows the use of electronic communications in dealings conducted under those conventions.

Domestically, the ECC can serve as a substitute for the Model Law on Electronic Commerce (MLEC), although it may still be useful to enact some of the MLES provisions. The ECC applies to cross-border contractual deals but needs only minor amendments to work as domestic law.

CAREC countries should also accede to the UN Framework Agreement on Facilitation of Cross-Border Paperless Trade in Asia and the Pacific (footnote 86). This agreement provides appropriate guidance for creating national law that complies with best practices for cross-border paperless trade. Accession also gives countries access to meetings and other resources where all member states collaborate on the policy and practical aspects of international e-commerce. The CAREC Program and members may explore collaboration with other efforts to reach arrangements on matters of international e-commerce, including those of the Eurasian Economic Union (EAEU) to develop a transboundary trust framework (footnote 93).

---

[275] It is difficult to say anything about the integrity of a document without verifying the results of the operation of a hash function, i.e., a mathematical processing of the data that produces a 'digital fingerprint' that can be used to ensure that a text has not been altered. Some people are skeptical that the characteristics of an MLES Article 6(3) signature can ever be thoroughly proved, which is why they prefer a specified technology solution with an independent verifier to certify that the technology has been properly applied.

Finally, CAREC countries should consider and explore how international conventions and guidelines may authorize the use of electronic communications. The legal opportunities may already exist in their national laws through their membership in these conventions, which means they need only take advantage of them. For example, the risk-management approach to customs clearances under the Revised Kyoto Convention, implemented in an electronic system, may help allay the concerns of customs authorities who fear the deluge of small-value shipments if residents increase their purchases of consumer items from abroad through electronic vendors like Alibaba or Amazon.[276]

Privacy

It is important to the growth of trust that the state be effective in enforcing personal privacy rights and prohibiting cybercrime. Legal protection can enhance the willingness of consumers to take a chance on the intangible medium of e-communications. Most CAREC countries' privacy laws are founded on sound principles. The statutes all prohibit the collection of personal data without the informed consent of the data subject, subject to such common exceptions as the collection of information that is already public knowledge. They nearly all give extra protection to sensitive kinds of information and have similar definitions of what these are. They all offer some degree of state enforcement of privacy rights. However, consumer trust will depend to some extent on how active and how credible this enforcement is. Most of the current statutes properly allow transfer of personal data abroad only if there is equivalent legislative protection, a relevant treaty with the destination country, or (sometimes) the consent of the data subject. Businesses operating in several countries, particularly online businesses, will appreciate being allowed to handle personal data, such as customer information, in one place with single or uniform standard.

Cybercrime

The CAREC countries' laws have generally followed the same model in preparing cybercrime legislation. They tend to have the same three provisions in the same order. Judging from the two international standards for such provisions—the Council of Europe Convention on Cybercrime (Budapest Convention of 2001) (footnote 33) and a draft treaty (footnote 35)—they cover the essentials. Given the rapid evolution of online technology—and of online crime—the CAREC countries should review their criminal legislation to ensure that they are capable of prosecuting offences listed in the international texts. To combat cybercrime properly, extensive cross-border collaboration will be needed, often over a long period.

---

[276] For a discussion on issues presented by large numbers of small packages, see Asian Development Bank (ADB). 2016. A Snapshot of E-Commerce in Central Asia. *Asian Development Blog.* 18 January. https://blogs.adb.org/blog/snapshot-e-commerce-central-asia. Further thoughts on the small package issue were set out by in the following: P. Jonasson. 2019. *Trade facilitation for e-commerce: Emerging innovations for seamless cross-border transactions. Panel presentation prepared for the Asia-Pacific Trade Facilitation Forum.* New Delhi. 17–18 September. https://www.unescap.org/sites/default/files/5.3%20-%20Panelists.pdf.

Consumer Protection

The everyday merchant or customer participating in e-commerce will benefit—and her or his trust will be enhanced—by well-designed consumer protection law. Nearly half the CAREC countries have consumer protection legislation that covers both online and offline transactions. The reluctance to adopt such statutes (in the past, at least) may have been partly because of state hesitation about interfering in the market through complaints bureaus, accessible dispute resolution by small claims courts and mediation, and educational programs. Those resources may not have been available then and providing them may be a low priority even now.[277] However, some countries may need to build their capacity to offer them. It is recommended that CAREC countries turn their minds to developing harmonized consumer protection legislation based on the UN's Guidelines for Consumer Protection Legislation and Organisation for Economic Co-operation and Development (OECD) principles (footnote 40). They should pay special attention to the experience of other countries, especially those with new legislation. It would certainly encourage e-commerce if merchants had the same duties to their customers wherever these customers were. A stronger argument can be made for harmonizing laws for online sales across CAREC countries than for offline ones.

The CAREC countries that are not already members should also consider joining the International Consumer Protection and Enforcement Network (footnote 51). Network information sharing is one of its prime benefits, since it enables states to be up to date on what the current risks to consumers are. Network membership can also help local enforcement authorities prevent illegal or damaging cross-border activity that originates outside their jurisdiction. A potential long-term project is to design a system of online dispute resolution for consumers in the region.

---

[277] The economies of several CAREC members depended for a long time on state-owned industries. In some cases, these states may have been reluctant to make the operations of those industries more complicated by giving rights to their customers.

8 Conclusion and Next Steps

Electronic commerce (e-commerce) is a complex and widespread phenomenon that spans the Central Asia Regional Economic Cooperation (CAREC) countries and the globe. Digital technologies are transforming economic activity, while the coronavirus disease (COVID-19) pandemic has led to greater reliance on online services and accelerated the pace of e-commerce. The study makes a case for modernization and potential harmonization of legislation of CAREC countries leveraging on international instruments and best practices, while recognizing that each country has its own legislative traditions, its own drafting style, and its own legal conventions. Development partners, such as the Asian Development Bank (ADB), the CAREC Institute, and United Nations (UN) agencies, have resources to help coordinate law reform among the CAREC members and beyond.

E-commerce involves and relates to the responsibilities of many parts of government and the private sector. Any effort at law reform should therefore engage a wide number of interested people and agencies (trade, customs, and information and communication technology departments at the minimum). At the national level, an interagency task force or coordinating council with a clear mandate and support at the highest level of government is recommended. For example, in Mongolia, a policy-making body under the auspices of the Prime Minister is responsible for developing and implementing policies related to communications and information technologies. It launched E-Mongolia, a single platform with digitalized government services, through a memorandum of understanding and cross-agency coordination. In the same vein, implementation of initiatives to promote e-commerce both on the demand and the supply side require similar arrangements, in Mongolia and in general.

Leveraging this research and to continuously support CAREC members, several ADB technical assistance projects are underway to deliver capacity building, including through training modules, regulatory sandboxes, or advisory support for domestic reforms.[278] It is crucial that the process of delivering legal advice to government be coordinated, whether it is provided by in-house legal staff or outside law firms. Private sector participation is also important. Those who will be affected by a reformed legal regime should have some input into the form it will take (including how it may relate to other legislation, for example in customs processes and single electronic windows for trade). A national working group on e-commerce law reform should be echoed by those dealing with international or cross-border e-commerce, closely coordinating with each other.

Promotion of e-commerce and innovation is an identified priority under the CAREC Integrated Trade Agenda 2030, which aims to create an enabling environment for economic diversification through reforms, financing, and countries' integration with global and regional value chains.[279] In particular, the agenda covers:

    (i)   digital trade promotion through knowledge-sharing on best practices and a framework on e-commerce,

---

[278] See ADB. 2019. Technical assistance for Implementing the Integrated Trade Agenda in the Central Asia Regional Economic Cooperation Program. Manila; ADB. 2019. Technical assistance for Better Customs for Better Client Services in Central Asia Regional Economic Cooperation Countries. Manila; ADB. 2021. Technical assistance for Enabling a Conducive Environment for the Digital Economy. Manila; ADB 2020. Technical assistance for Supporting Startup Ecosystem in the Central Asia Regional Economic Cooperation Region to Mitigate Impact of COVID-19 and Support Economic Revival. Manila.

[279] Footnote 2.

(ii)   a scoping study on adoption of e-commerce and innovation in government services related to trade,

(iii)   a pilot initiative on the new Framework of Standards for Cross-Border E-Commerce of the World Customs Organization (WCO)[280] and

(iv)   support to the Enabling E-Commerce Initiative of the World Trade Organization (WTO) (footnote 74).

Harmonization to the extent possible among CAREC members will greatly increase the value of their e-commerce law reforms and reduce their workload in keeping e-commerce law up to date. The CAREC countries may benefit from even broader cooperation if they choose to participate in policy dialogues and expert groups such as the United Nations Network of Experts for Paperless Trade and Transport in Asia and the Pacific (UNNExT) (footnote 89). Countries that are going to make the effort to update and harmonize their laws to increase public and business confidence in the safety of e-commerce should and need to find out what the current state of such law is from the accessible sources in Asia and across the world. Knowing what law is in force elsewhere and what is not would be extremely valuable. This knowledge should be gained from such sources as national statutes and regulations and other implementing texts.[281]

Law is part of a nation's economic infrastructure, just as real and important as roads and telecommunications and ports. Law needs to be modernized, just as physical infrastructure does. And law, like roads and other infrastructure, needs to accompany trade across borders. The world is not coming fresh to electronic commerce. Major intergovernmental bodies and global and regional private sector entities have been studying appropriate responses to the challenges of e-communication for decades. There is a good deal of consensus on the responses this study has examined as they may apply to the 11 diverse countries of the CAREC Program. The CAREC countries have all been dealing with electronic commerce in their laws. This study recommends a coordinated effort to bring their laws as close to the global consensus as their social cultures and the stages of their economic development will allow.

Moving forward, the CAREC Regional Trade Group, which is the lead coordinative and consultative body for overarching issues, together with the CAREC Customs Cooperation Committee, can be suitable platforms for (i) policy dialogue to promote harmonization of laws and mutual recognition, (ii) cross-learning to share experience and information especially among experts, and (iii) promotion of cross-border connectivity and interoperability through customs agencies' cooperation and private sector e-platforms. A broader CAREC Digital Strategy 2030 will help accelerate digital transformation in the region, which will complement existing efforts to develop e-commerce ecosystem and promote digital trade.

---

[280]   World Customs Organization, 2018. Framework of Standards for Cross-Border E-Commerce of the World Customs Organization. http://www.wcoomd.org/-/media/wco/public/global/pdf/topics/facilitation/activities-and-programmes/ecommerce/wco-framework-of-standards-on-crossborder-ecommerce_en.pdf?la=en.

[281]   Several CAREC members have their statutes or part of them online. However, the status, effect, or subordinate instruments of these statutes are not equally easy to determine from these online versions. Ideally, the collective texts would be made available in English, Chinese, and Russian languages.

APPENDIX:
Overview of E-Commerce-Related Legislation in Central Asia Regional Economic Cooperation Countries

Legislation	Afghanistan	Azerbaijan	People's Republic of China	Georgia	Kazakhstan	Kyrgyz Republic	Mongolia	Pakistan	Tajikistan	Turkmenistan	Uzbekistan
E-transactions	*	•	•	•	•	•	•	•	•	•	•
E-documents	*	•	•	•	•	•	•	•	•	•	•
E-signatures	*	•	•	•	•	•	•	•	•	•	•
International certificates and foreign signatures	*	•	•	•	•	•	•	•	•	•	•
Privacy	*	•	•	•	•	•	*	*	•	•	•
Cybercrime	•	•	•	•	o	o	o	•	o	o	o
Consumer Protection	•	•	•	o	•	o	•	*	*	•	o

• = specific legislation or modern statutes are available that are generally compliant with international instruments (with minimum provisions applicable to e-commerce transactions).

o = there is no specific legislation but there is general legislation (such as civil or criminal codes) that is applicable to all kinds of transactions and is considered media-neutral legislation or statutes.

* = there is incomplete legislation, outdated provisions, or a law has yet to be enacted.

Source: Author's compilation.

References

African Union. 2014. *African Union Convention on Cybersecurity and Personal Data Protection*. https://au.int/sites/default/files/treaties/29560-treaty-0048_-_african_union_convention_on_cyber_security_and_personal_data_protection_e.pdf.

Asian Development Bank (ADB). 2016. A Snapshot of E-Commerce in Central Asia. *Asian Development Blog*. 18 January. https://blogs.adb.org/blog/snapshot-e-commerce-central-asia.

ADB. 2019. Technical assistance for Implementing the Integrated Trade Agenda in the Central Asia Regional Economic Cooperation Program. Manila.

ADB. 2019. Technical assistance for Better Customs for Better Client Services in Central Asia Regional Economic Cooperation Countries. Manila.

ADB. 2021. Technical assistance for Enabling a Conducive Environment for the Digital Economy. Manila.

ADB 2020. Technical assistance for Supporting Startup Ecosystem in the Central Asia Regional Economic Cooperation Region to Mitigate Impact of COVID-19 and Support Economic Revival. Manila.

ADB and United Nations (UN) Economic and Social Commission for Asia and the Pacific (ESCAP). 2018. *Embracing the E-Commerce Revolution in Asia and the Pacific*. Manila. https://www.adb.org/sites/default/files/publication/430401/embracing-e-commerce-revolution.pdf.

Council of Europe. 2001. *Convention on Cybercrime*. https://www.coe.int/en/web/conventions/full-list/-/conventions/rms/0900001680081561.

————. 1981. *Convention for the Protection of Individuals with regard to Automatic Processing of Personal Data*. https://www.coe.int/en/web/conventions/full-list/-/conventions/treaty/108.

————. 2018. *Modernised Convention for the Protection of Individuals with Regard to the Processing of Personal Data*. https://www.coe.int/en/web/data-protection/convention108/modernised.

Convention on International Trade in Endangered Species of Wild Fauna and Flora. 1973 (amended 1979 and 1983). Convention text. https://cites.org/eng/disc/text.php.

Y. Duval and K. Mengjing. 2017. Digital Trade Facilitation: Paperless Trade in Regional Trade Agreements. *ADB Institute Working Paper Series*. No. 747. Tokyo: ADB Institute. https://www.adb.org/sites/default/files/publication/321851/adbi-wp747.pdf.

ESCAP. 2019. *Framework Agreement on Facilitation of Cross-Border Paperless Trade in Asia and the Pacific.* Bangkok. https://www.unescap.org/sites/default/files/UNESCAP%20Framework%20Agreement%20e-book.pdf.

———. 2019. *Readiness Assessment for Cross-Border Paperless Trade: Mongolia.* Bangkok. https://www.unescap.org/sites/default/d8files/knowledge-products/MNG-CBPT%20 readiness%20assessment%20report-FINAL%2B.pdf.

———. 2019. *Readiness Assessment for Cross-Border Paperless Trade: Uzbekistan.* https://www.unescap.org/sites/default/d8files/knowledge-products/UZB-CBPT%20Readiness-FINAL%2B.pdf.

———. 2019. *Digital and Sustainable Trade Facilitation in Central Asia Regional Economic Cooperation.* https://www.unescap.org/sites/default/d8files/knowledge-products/UNTF%20CAREC%20Report%20 %282019.12.27%29.pdf.

Economic Commission for Latin America and the Caribbean. 2015. Q&A: ECLAC participates in regional E-Commerce workshop. *The Hummingbird.* 2 (11). https://repositorio.cepal.org/bitstream/ handle/11362/41984/1/HummingbirdNovember2015.pdf.

European Union (EU). 2019. *Directive as regards the better enforcement and modernization of European Union consumer protection rules.* https://data.consilium.europa.eu/doc/document/PE-83-2019-INIT/en/pdf.

Government of the United States, Department of Commerce, International Trade Administration.

   https://www.export.gov/apex/article2?id=Azerbaijan-ecommerce

   https://www.export.gov/apex/article2?id=China-ecommerce

   https://www.export.gov/apex/article2?id=Mongolia-Ecommerce

   https://www.export.gov/apex/article2?id=Kyrgyz-Republic-Ecommerce

   https://www.trade.gov/knowledge-product/pakistan-ecommerce

   https://www.export.gov/apex/article2?id=Tajikistan-Ecommerce

   https://www.export.gov/apex/article2?id=Turkmenistan-Ecommerce

   https://www.export.gov/apex/article2?id=Uzbekistan-Ecommerce

J. Gregory. 2014. Legislating Trust, *Canadian Journal of Law and Technology.* 12 (1). https://digitalcommons. schulichlaw.dal.ca/cjlt/vol12/iss1/1/.

———. 2017. Proprietary Algorithms for Public Purposes. *Slaw.* http://www.slaw.ca/2017/07/24/proprietary-algorithms-for-public-purposes/.

———. 2018. Trade Agreements to Promote E-Commerce II. *Slaw.* http://www.slaw.ca/2018/11/08/trade-agreements-to-promote-electronic-commerce-ii/.

———. 2019. Trade Agreements to Promote E-Commerce III. *Slaw.* http://www.slaw.ca/2019/12/30/trade-agreements-to-promote-electronic-commerce-iii/

Y. Ismail. 2020. *E-commerce in the World Trade Organization: History and latest developments in the negotiations under the Joint Statement.* Negotiating brief prepared for the Geneva Seminar: Joint Statement Initiative on Electronic Commerce. Geneva. 29 January. https://www.iisd.org/system/files/publications/e-commerce-world-trade-organization-.pdf.

F. Kamali. 2017. Afghanistan's Cybercrime law – digital watchdog or another futile ambitious effort. *Pajhwok Afghan News*. 7 June. https://www.pajhwok.com/en/opinions/afghanistan%E2%80%99s-cyber-crime-law-digital-watchdog-or-another-futile-ambitious-effort.

S. Mason. 2017. *A Convention on Electronic Evidence: helping to provide for certainty in international trade*. The full text is available at https://www.researchgate.net/publication/309878298_Draft_Convention_on_Electronic_Evidence.

J. Monteiro and R. Teh. 2017. Provisions on Electronic Commerce in Regional Trade Agreements. *WTO Working Papers*. No. ERSD-2017-11. Geneva: World Trade Organization (WTO) Economic Research and Statistics Division. https://www.wto.org/english/res_e/reser_e/ersd201711_e.pdf.

Organisation for Economic Co-operation and Development (OECD). 1980 (amended 2013). *Guidelines on the Protection of Privacy and Transborder Flows of Personal Data*. https://www.oecd.org/internet/ieconomy/oecdguidelinesontheprotectionofprivacyandtransborderfl owsofpersonaldata.htm.

———. 1999. *Guidelines for Consumer Protection in the Context of Electronic Commerce*. https://www.oecd.org/sti/consumer/oecdguidelinesforconsumerprotectioninthecontextofelectroniccommer.

———. 2016. Consumer Protection in E-commerce: OECD Recommendation, OECD Publishing, Paris, http://dx.doi.org/10.1787/9789264255258-en. https://www.oecd.org/sti/consumer/Ecommerce-Recommendation-2016.pdf.

———. 2013. *The OECD Privacy Framework*. https://www.oecd.org/sti/ieconomy/oecd_privacy_framework.pdf.

Pasadilla. 2020. E-commerce provisions in RTAs: Implications for negotiations and capacity building. *Asia-Pacific Research and Training Network on Trade Working Papers*. No. 192. Bangkok: ESCAP. https://www.unescap.org/sites/default/files/AWP192%20Pasadilla%20Gloria_2.pdf.

Peters. 2019. Russia and China are trying to set the U.N.'s Rules on Cybercrime. *Foreign Policy*. 16 September. https://foreignpolicy.com/2019/09/16/russia-and-china-are-trying-to-set-the-u-n-s-rules-on-cybercrime/.

Richard and P. Quah. 2019. Where are we now with data protection law in China? *Freshfields Bruckhaus Deringer Digital blog*. 11 September. https://digital.freshfields.com/post/102fqnd/where-are-we-now-with-data-protection-law-in-china-updated-september-2019

Stalbovskaya (update by M. Khasanov). 2019. A Guide to Legal Research in Uzbekistan. *GlobaLex*. http://www.nyulawglobal.org/globalex/Uzbekistan1.html.

United Nations Commission on International Trade Law (UNCITRAL). 1980. *United Nations Convention on Contracts for the International Sale of Goods*. Vienna. https://www.uncitral.org/pdf/english/texts/sales/cisg/V1056997-CISG-e-book.pdf.

———. 1996. *Model Law on Electronic Commerce*. Vienna. https://uncitral.un.org/en/texts/ecommerce/modellaw/electronic_commerce

———. 2001. *Model Law on Electronic Signatures*. Vienna. https://uncitral.un.org/en/texts/ecommerce/modellaw/electronic_signatures.

———. 2005. Convention on the Use of Electronic Communications in International Contracts ("Electronic Communications Convention"). https://uncitral.un.org/en/texts/ecommerce/conventions/electronic_communications.

———. 2017. *UNCITRAL Model Law on Electronic Transferable Records*. Vienna. https://uncitral.un.org/en/texts/ecommerce/modellaw/electronic_transferable_records.

UN Conference on Trade and Development (UNCTAD). 2019. *Rapid eTrade Readiness Assessment of Least Developed Countries: Policy Impact and Way Forward*. https://unctad.org/en/PublicationsLibrary/dtlstict2019d7_en.pdf.

———. *United Nations Guidelines for Consumer Protection*. Geneva. https://unctad.org/en/PublicationsLibrary/ditccplpmisc2016d1_en.pdf.

———. 2018. UNCTAD's Estimates of Global E-commerce 2018. *UNCTAD Technical Notes on ICT for Development*. No. 15. https://unctad.org/system/files/official-document/tn_unctad_ict4d15_en.pdf.

———. 2019. UNCTAD B2C E-Commerce Index 2019. *UNCTAD Technical Notes on ICT for Development*. No. 14. https://unctad.org/system/files/official-document/tn_unctad_ict4d14_en.pdf.

———. 2019. *Afghanistan Rapid eTrade Readiness Assessment*. Geneva. https://unctad.org/en/PublicationsLibrary/dtlstict2019d5_en.pdf.

UN Centre for Trade Facilitation and Electronic Business (UN/CEFACT). 2014. *Revision of Recommendation 14: Authentication of Trade Documents*. Geneva. https://www.unece.org/fileadmin/DAM/cefact/recommendations/rec14/ECE_TRADE_C_CEFACT_2014_6E_Rec14.pdf.

United Nations Economic Commission for Europe (UNECE). 1982 (amended 2008 and 2011). *International Convention on the Harmonization of Frontier Controls of Goods*. Geneva. http://www.unece.org/fileadmin/DAM/trans/conventn/ECE-TRANS-55r2e.pdf.

UN. 2019. *Digital and Sustainable Trade Facilitation: Global Report 2019*. https://www.unescap.org/sites/default/d8files/knowledge-products/Untfsurvey%20global%20report%202019.pdf.

Universal Postal Union. 2020. *Postal Development Report 2020*. https://www.upu.int/UPU/media/upu/publications/2020-Postal-Development-Report.pdf.

World Customs Organization (WCO). 2008. *Revised Kyoto Convention*. Brussels. http://www.wcoomd.org/en/topics/facilitation/instrument-andtools/conventions/pf_revised_kyoto_conv/kyoto_new.aspx.

World Economic Forum. 2020. Advancing Digital Trade in Asia. Community Paper. October 2020. Geneva. https://www.weforum.org/reports/advancing-digital-trade-in-asia

WTO. 2020. *E-Commerce, Trade and the COVID-19 Pandemic: Information Note*. Geneva. https://www.wto.org/english//tratop_e/covid19_e/ecommerce_report_e.pdf.

Databases:

Groupe Société Générale. Import Export Solutions. Country Profiles. https://import-export.societegenerale.fr/en/country. (accessed 5 August 2020).

International Telecommunications Union. Country ICT Data. https://www.itu.int/en/ITU-D/Statistics/Pages/stat/default.aspx (accessed 5 August 2020).

Global System for Mobile Communications Association. Mobile Connectivity Index 2019. https://www.mobileconnectivityindex.com/ (accessed 1 August 2020).

Speedtest Global Index. https://www.speedtest.net/global-index (accessed 11 June 2020).

World Bank. World Development Indicators. https://databank.worldbank.org/source/world-development-indicators (accessed 1 August 2020).

World Bank. Global Findex database. https://globalfindex.worldbank.org/#data_sec_focus (accessed 2 August 2020).

World Bank. Logistics Performance Index 2018. https://lpi.worldbank.org/international/global (accessed 2 August 2020).

World Economic Forum. Networked Readiness Index 2019. https://reports.weforum.org/global-information-technology-report-2016/networked-readiness-index/ (accessed 2 August 2020).

Laws:

Government of Afghanistan, Ministry of Industry and Commerce. Competition Promotion and Consumer Protection. https://moci.gov.af/en/competition-promotion-and-consumer-protection.

Government of Afghanistan, Ministry of Justice. 2016. *Law on Consumer Protection* (in Pashto and Dari). Kabul http://old.moj.gov.af/Content/files/OfficialGazette/01201/OG_01241.pdf.

Government of the United States, Library of Congress. 2017. Afghanistan: Cyber Crime Code Signed into Law. News release. 16 August. https://www.loc.gov/law/foreign-news/article/afghanistan-cyber-crime-code-signed-into-law/.

Government of Azerbaijan. 1995 (amended 2019). *Law of the Azerbaijan Republic about Consumer Protection*. Baku. https://cis-legislation.com/document.fwx?rgn=2795.

Government of Azerbaijan. 2004 (amended 2008 and 2016). *Law of the Azerbaijan Republic about the Digital Signature and the Electronic Document*. Baku. http://cis-legislation.com/document.fwx?rgn=7428.

Government of Azerbaijan. 2010 (amended 2018). *Law of the Azerbaijan Republic about Personal Data*. Baku. http://cis-legislation.com/document.fwx?rgn=31412.

Government of Azerbaijan. 2005 (amended 2018). *Law of the Azerbaijan Republic about Electronic Trading*. Baku. http://cis-legislation.com/document.fwx?rgn=9111.

Government of the PRC. 1980 (as amended 1997). Criminal Law of the People's Republic of China. https://www.fmprc.gov.cn/ce/cgvienna/eng/dbtyw/jdwt/crimelaw/.

Government of the PRC. 2019. *Electronic Signature Law of the People's Republic of China*. Beijing. http://pkulaw.cn/fulltext_form.aspx?Gid=331476&Db=chl (in Chinese).

Government of the PRC. 2019. *E-Commerce Law of the People's Republic of China*. Beijing. http://pkulaw.cn/fulltext_form.aspx?Gid=321035&Db=chl (in Chinese).

Government of the PRC. 2013. *Law of the People's Republic of China on the Protection of Consumer Rights and Interests*. Beijing. http://pkulaw.cn/fulltext_form.aspx?Gid=211792 (in Chinese).

Government of Georgia. 2017. *Law of Georgia on Electronic Documents and Electronic Trust Services*. Tbilisi. https://matsne.gov.ge/en/document/view/3654557?publication=0.

Government of Georgia. 2016. *Law of Georgia on Personal Data Protection*. Tbilisi. https://matsne.gov.ge/en/document/view/1561437?publication=9.

Government of Kazakhstan. 1997. *Law of the Republic of Kazakhstan No. 168 on Introduction of the Criminal Code of the Republic of Kazakhstan*. Nur-Sultan. https://adilet.zan.kz/eng/docs/K970000167.

Government of Kazakhstan. 2003 (amended 2020). *Law of the Republic of Kazakhstan About the Electronic Document and Electronic Digital Signature*. Nur-Sultan. http://cis-legislation.com/document.fwx?rgn=3148.

Government of Kazakhstan. 2013 (amended 2020). *Law of the Republic of Kazakhstan about Personal Data and their Protection*. Nur-Sultan. http://cis-legislation.com/document.fwx?rgn=59981.

Government of Kazakhstan. 2015 (amended 2020). *Law of the Republic of Kazakhstan about Informatization*. Nur-Sultan. http://cis-legislation.com/document.fwx?rgn=80847.

Government of Kazakhstan. 2010 (amended 2020). *Law of the Republic of Kazakhstan about Consumer Protection*. Nur-Sultan. https://cis-legislation.com/document.fwx?rgn=31140.

Government of the Kyrgyz Republic. 1997 (as amended). *Criminal Code of the Kyrgyz Republic*. Bishkek. http://www.ilo.org/dyn/natlex/docs/ELECTRONIC/67156/104401/F1696552027/KGZ67156%20Eng.pdf (Unofficial translation).

Government of the Kyrgyz Republic. 2017 (amended 2020). *Law of the Kyrgyz Republic about Electronic Control*. Bishkek. http://cis-legislation.com/document.fwx?rgn=99015.

Government of the Kyrgyz Republic. 2008 (amended 2017). *Law of the Kyrgyz Republic about Information of Personal Nature*. Bishkek. https://cis-legislation.com/document.fwx?rgn=22274#A000000012.

Government of the Kyrgyz Republic. 2020. *Order No. 233 about authorized bodies of the Kyrgyz Republic on confirmation of electronic documents in case of cross-border information exchange of subjects of electronic interaction*. Bishkek. https://cis-legislation.com/document.fwx?rgn=124656.

Government of the Kyrgyz Republic. 2020. *Order No. 266 about some questions in the field of ensuring cyber security*. Bishkek. https://cis-legislation.com/document.fwx?rgn=124892.

Government of the Kyrgyz Republic. 1997 (as amended to date). *Law on the Protection of Consumer Rights.* http://cbd.minjust.gov.kg/act/view/ru-ru/590 (in Russian).

Government of Mongolia, Communications Regulatory Commission. 2011. *Law of Mongolia on Electronic Signature.* http://www.crc.gov.mn/en/k/2lq/1q.

Government of Mongolia. 1995. *Law about Personal Secrets.* Ulaanbaatar. https://www.legalinfo.mn/law/details/537 (in Mongolian).

Government of Mongolia, 2003. Law on Consumer Protection (as amended in 2015). Ulaanbaatar. https://www.legalinfo.mn/law/details/551 (in Mongolian).

Government of Mongolia. 2011. *Law of Mongolia About Electronic Signatures* (as amended in 2018). Ulaanbaatar. https://www.legalinfo.mn/law/details/574?lawid=574. (in Mongolian).

Government of Mongolia. 2013. *Criminal Code of Mongolia* (as amended in 2018). Ulaanbaatar. https://www.legalinfo.mn/law/details/15901?lawid=15901.

Government of Pakistan. 2002. *Electronic Transactions Ordinance.* Islamabad. https://www.ecac.org.pk/assets/front/files/eto2002.pdf.

Government of Pakistan, Ministry of Information Technology and Telecom, Electronic Certification Accreditation Council (ECAC). 2008. The Certification Service Providers' Accreditation Regulations, 2008. Islamabad. https://www.ecac.org.pk/assets/front/files/The%20Certification%20Service%20Providers'%20Accreditation%20Regulations,%202008%20updated.pdf.

Government of Pakistan. 2016. *An Act to make provisions for prevention of electronic crimes.* Islamabad. http://www.na.gov.pk/uploads/documents/1462252100_756.pdf.

Government of Pakistan, Commerce Division. 2019. *E-Commerce Policy of Pakistan.* Islamabad. http://www.commerce.gov.pk/wp-content/uploads/2019/11/e-Commerce_Policy_of_Pakistan_Print.pdf.

Provincial Assembly of Sindh. 2015. *The Sindh Consumer Protection Act, 2014.* Karachi. http://www.pas.gov.pk/index.php/acts/details/en/31/284.

Government of Tajikistan.1998 (amended 2020), *Criminal Code of Tajikistan.* Dushanbe. https://cis-legislation.com/document.fwx?rgn=2324.

Government of Tajikistan. 2002 (amended 2014). *Law of the Republic of Tajikistan about Electronic Documents.* Dushanbe. http://cis-legislation.com/document.fwx?rgn=2183.

Government of Tajikistan. 2007 (amended 2011). *Law of the Republic of Tajikistan about the Electronic Digital Signature.* Dushanbe. http://cis-legislation.com/document.fwx?rgn=18412.

Government of Turkmenistan. 2020. *Law of Turkmenistan about the Electronic Document, Electronic Document Management and Digital Services.* Ashgabat. https://cis-legislation.com/document.fwx?rgn=123179.

Government of Uzbekistan. 1994 (amended 2020) *Criminal Code of the Republic of Uzbekistan.* Tashkent. https://lex.uz/docs/111457.

Government of Uzbekistan. 1996 (amended 2019). *Law about Consumer Protection.* Tashkent. https://cis-legislation.com/document.fwx?rgn=909

Government of Uzbekistan. 2003 (amended 2018). *Law about Electronic Digital Signatures.* Tashkent. http://cis-legislation.com/document.fwx?rgn=11889.

Government of Uzbekistan. 2004 (amended 2017). *Law about Electronic Commerce.* Tashkent. http://cis-legislation.com/document.fwx?rgn=6591.

Government of Uzbekistan. 2004. *Law about Electronic Document Management.* Tashkent. http://cis-legislation.com/document.fwx?rgn=6592.

Government of the Republic of Uzbekistan. 2004. *Law about Informatization* (as amended, 2021). Tashkent. https://lex.uz/docs/82956.

Government of Uzbekistan. 2015. *Law about the Electronic Government.* Tashkent. http://cis-legislation.com/document.fwx?rgn=81271.

Government of Uzbekistan. 2016 (amended 2018). *Resolution No. 185 of the Cabinet of Ministers of the Republic of Uzbekistan about measures for further enhancement of procedure of transactions in electronic commerce.* Tashkent. http://cis-legislation.com/document.fwx?rgn=86244.

Government of Uzbekistan. 2019. *Law about Personal Data.* Tashkent. http://cis-legislation.com/document.fwx?rgn=116961.